RON MILLER

MARS

WORLDS BEYOND

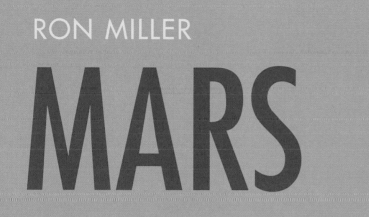

TF
CB
TWENTY-FIRST CENTURY BOOKS

MINNEAPOLIS

Dedicated to Tyler Durant and Ryan Durant

Illustrations and text copyright © 2006 by Ron Miller
Photographs courtesy of NASA

Twenty-First Century Books
A division of Lerner Publishing Group
241 First Avenue North
Minneapolis, Minnesota 55401 U.S.A.

Website address: www.lernerbooks.com

Library of Congress Cataloging-in-Publication Data

Miller, Ron, 1947–
   Mars / Ron Miller.
     p.   cm. — (Worlds beyond)
   Summary: Chronicles the discovery and explorations of the planet Mars
 and discusses each of its moons, its place in the solar system, and more.
 Includes bibliographical references and index.
   ISBN 0-7613-2362-7 (lib. bdg.)
   1. Mars (Planet)—Juvenile literature. [1. Mars (Planet)] I. Title.
   QB641 .M54 2006
   523.43—dc21   2003010139

Manufactured in the United States of America
1 2 3 4 5 6 – DP – 11 10 09 08 07 06

CONTENTS

Astronomical symbol for Mars

CHAPTER ONE

THE RED PLANET

For thousands of years, people have been intrigued by the bright red "star" that blazes in the night sky for a few months every other year. The color reminded many ancient civilizations of war, fire, and blood. The Egyptians called the star Harmarkhis. To the Chaldeans it was Nergal, the same name as the god of battle and of the dead. The Persians named it Pahlavani Siphir, the Celestial Warrior. To the Greeks it was Ares, which meant disaster and vengeance. The Romans called the star Mars, for the god of war. (Even the astronomical symbol for Mars is derived from a warrior's shield and spear.)

These ancient civilizations noticed that the red star and four others were very unusual. All of the other stars remained in the same positions relative to one another from night to night, month to month, and year to year, but these other five stars *moved*. Because they appeared to wander across the sky, they were called *planets*, from the Greek word *planetes*, which means "wanderer."

It took many thousands of years for humans to progress from the idea of a supernatural being—a dimensionless, nonmaterial

(5)

spot of light in the sky—to the concept of "sister planet," a world perhaps much like our own. Although most of the discoveries about the true nature of Mars have taken place in the last three hundred years, the groundwork was laid much earlier.

Early Observations

The Greek scientist Aristotle (384–322 B.C.) happened to observe Mars pass behind the Moon of Earth and deduced that Mars must be farther away than the Moon. At this time, Mars was still considered just another light in the sky, like the rest of the stars, but Aristotle's discovery was a small step toward learning the planet's true nature. The next step, however, took much longer. It was nearly two thousand years before anyone realized that Mars was a world in its own right.

In 1608, a Dutch spectacle-maker named Hans Lippershey invented the telescope. The Italian scientist Galileo Galilei (1564–1642) heard of this wonderful device and, after some experimentation, made one for himself. One of Galileo's first intentions was to turn the telescope toward the night sky. In doing this, he immediately made a fundamental discovery: Seen through a telescope, the stars still looked like simple points of light, but the planets showed disks. Since they had shapes, this meant that the planets must be *objects*. People could still argue about the stars, Galileo realized, but the planets were actually *bodies*, similar to Earth.

But Galileo's telescope was too small to reveal any details on Mars. The first person to sketch any recognizable features was

In many mythologies, the planet Mars is represented by the god of war.

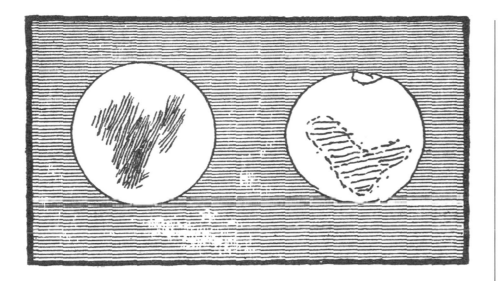

This 1659 sketch of Mars by Christian Huygens was the first to show recognizable features, including one of the polar caps.

Christian Huygens (1629–1695), the son of a Dutch diplomat and poet, who had a much better telescope than the Italian scientist. A dedicated physicist and mathematician, Huygens made drawings of Mars between 1659 and 1683 that show features easily recognizable today. In fact, he was the first to clearly show the south polar cap.

Other astronomers were able to estimate the length of the Martian day by observing the movements of the planet's features as it rotated, but little was added to the general knowledge of Mars until the end of the eighteenth century. That was when one of the greatest observers of the century, William Herschel (1738–1822), the discoverer of Uranus, turned his attention to the red planet.

Although Herschel was an excellent observer, his drawings of Mars are little better than scribbles. But with the superior instru-

William Herschel

ments that were available to him, he made the first accurate measurements of the tilt of Mars's **axis** (which determines its seasons) and the length of its day. Both measurements were very similar to that of Earth. Earth's tilt is 23.45°, while Mars's tilt is 25.19°, and the length of Earth's day is 23.9 hours, while Mars's day is 24.6 hours. The days on Mars would seem familiar to a visitor from Earth, but because a year on Mars is twice as long as one on Earth, the seasons there would be twice as long as their terrestrial counterparts.

Herschel also expressed his belief that the white spots at the poles of Mars were ice and snow, similar to the polar caps of Earth, and that Mars had an atmosphere. He was even the first to observe color changes on Mars—a fact that would strongly influence late nineteenth-century theories about the red planet.

CHAPTER TWO

THE MEN OF MARS

Mars was fairly well known by the middle of the nineteenth century. Its size, length of day, and orbit had been precisely measured. It was known to be a planet of red deserts and dusky markings that seemed permanent enough to justify making maps, however much astronomers may have bickered over details. (What they bickered about even more were the *names* given to the features. British astronomer Richard Proctor angered his international colleagues by assigning the names of famous British astronomers to the largest, most prominent features on his map of Mars.)

Mars was also known to have polar caps of either carbon dioxide (CO_2) or ice and a thin atmosphere of uncertain composition. Although some astronomers had their doubts, the majority believed that the light, orange-colored regions were vast deserts and the dark, gray-green areas probably seas or marshes.

Great Discoveries

It wasn't until 1877 that another major discovery was made about Mars—or, to be accurate, two major discoveries. Astronomers hadn't

This nineteenth-century map of Mars illustrates the commonly held belief that the dark areas were oceans and lakes. The features on the map are all named after famous astronomers, a decision that caused a great deal of controversy since the astronomer who created the map was British and gave all the most prominent features the names of British scientists. It was quickly decided to revert to the classical names that had been used during the preceding centuries, most of which are still in use today.

been ignoring the planet until then, but nothing fundamentally *new* had been discovered. A great deal of their work was devoted either to creating ever more detailed (and often contradictory) maps of the planet or to refining measurements of its orbit and rotation. One thing was almost universally agreed upon: Mars had no moons.

Many astronomers had searched for moons around the red planet, but to no avail. One of the reasons they were eager to do so was that the orbit of a moon allows the mass of a planet to be calculated accurately. Even the great Herschel had conducted an unsuccessful search. But Asaph Hall, the professor of mathematics at the Naval Observatory in Washington, D.C., as he later said, was "tired of reading that Mars had no moons," and decided to look for moons himself.

After weeks of fruitless searching, Hall was beginning to agree with his predecessors and had decided to give up. His wife, however, insisted that he keep trying. Mars, she argued, would not be so close to Earth again for many years and if he had to report a negative result, well, at least that would be useful. So Hall went back to his telescope.

On the nights of August 15, 16, 20, and 21, he found two tiny pinpoints of light, nearly lost in the glare of the planet itself. He had finally discovered the moons of Mars! At the suggestion of an English correspondent, he named them Phobos and Deimos—fear and terror, the attendants of the god Mars.

The second great discovery made in 1877 had ramifications that lasted well into the twentieth century. Giovanni Schiaparelli, of the Brera Observatory in Milan, Italy, announced that he'd seen

The god Mars depicted in a nineteenth-century illustration is accompanied by his attendants, Phobos (fear) and Deimos (terror), for whom the planet's moons are named.

Giovanni Schiaparelli
Right: One of Schiaparelli's early maps of Mars, in which he depicted the many linear features he called "canali."

the surface of Mars crisscrossed by a network of thin lines. This would have been interesting enough, but it was what he *called* these lines that created international interest. The word he used was *canali*. In Italian, this means simply "channels" or "grooves," but it is so close to the English word *canal* that everyone assumed that's what Schiaparelli was referring to. The only difference—and it was a vital one—was that *canali* could describe a natural feature, but *canal* refers only to a man-made structure.

The debates started immediately. On one side were the astronomers who couldn't see any "canals" on Mars and said they didn't exist. On the other side were those who said they saw them and that they did exist. The latter group quickly divided itself into two camps: those who thought that the "canals" were natural features of some kind and those who thought they were artificial. (It might be worth mentioning that very few professional atronomers,

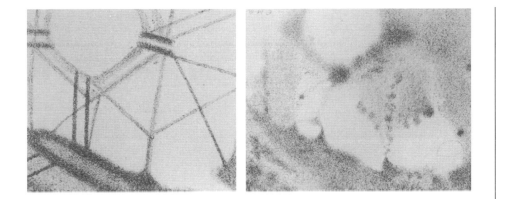

During the late nineteenth century, astronomers hotly debated the existence of canals on Mars. Most experienced professional astronomers dismissed them as mere optical illusions. On the left is a region drawn by Schiaparelli between 1877 and 1890. On the right is the same region as seen in 1909 to 1926 by E. M. Antoniadi, an Italian astronomer who was a staunch opponent of the canal theory. Where others had seen sharp lines, he saw only vague, broken-up details.

those working with the largest, best telescopes in the world, ever saw the canals. Even Asaph Hall, whose sharp eyes could pick out the tiny moons of Mars, never saw any canals.)

This is when Percival Lowell came onto the scene.

Lowell was born on March 13, 1855, to a wealthy family from Boston. He received a degree from Harvard and devoted himself to family business interests. In 1893, Lowell decided to take up observational astronomy after hearing that Schiaparelli was losing his eyesight and would no longer be able to continue his study of Mars. The next year, after extensive site testing, Lowell established a new observatory in Flagstaff, Arizona. One of its chief goals was to study Mars.

Lowell's maps of Mars looked like nothing else anyone had ever seen. They were covered with a network of fine, sharp lines that looked as artificial as modern maps of airline routes. He wrote two best-sellers about the planet: *Mars* (1895) and *Mars as the Abode of Life* (1908). The latter title pretty much summed up

Percival Lowell

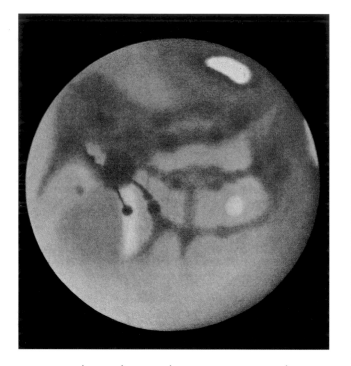

Mars as drawn by an observer in 1909: This was about as good a view of Mars as was possible until the advent of space travel.

his feelings about the nature of the "canals." He firmly believed them to be artificial structures built by intelligent, living beings.

"We saw," Lowell wrote, "how badly off for water Mars, to all appearance, is; so badly off that inhabitants of that other world would have to irrigate to live. . . . How to procure water enough to support life would be the great communal problem of the day." This is how Lowell imagined Mars—an ancient, desert world, much older than Earth, that had lost most of the water it might have once had. In desperation, Lowell presumed, the Martians had dug a vast system of enormous canals to carry water from the polar caps, when they melted in the summer, to the central regions of the planet. Lowell never claimed that he could actually see the canals—they would have to be many miles wide to be seen from Earth. Instead, he suggested that what was seen from Earth was the vegetation that grew along the canals, very much like the agricultural areas that abut the Nile River in Egypt.

Very few astronomers took Lowell's ideas seriously, but the public embraced them enthusiastically. A kind of "Mars fever" swept the world. Everything from novels and magazine articles to plays and fairground rides were inspired by the idea that there might be life on Mars. One notable author impressed by Lowell's theory was H. G. Wells, who was inspired to write the classic science fiction novel *The War of the Worlds* (1898). Others include Edgar Rice Burroughs (author of the Tarzan series), who wrote fabulous adventures about a Lowellian Mars inhabited by giant four-armed green Martian warriors and beautiful red princesses, and Ray Bradbury, who wrote such classics as *The Martian Chronicles* (1950).

Human eyes are designed to find meaningful patterns in random shapes. Do your eyes find a recognizable figure in the shapes above?

We know today that there are no canals on Mars like Percival Lowell, and many other observers, thought they saw. So what, then, did Lowell see? Most astronomers think that Lowell's canals were a combination of optical illusion and wishful thinking. Mars, at best, is a difficult object to observe: It is small and covered with a bewildering mass of fine detail.

The human eye and mind always try to find order in random patterns. If you were to toss a handful of pebbles on the floor, you would automatically start looking for patterns and relationships among them. Think of all the times you may have seen familiar shapes in clouds or found "faces" in cracks, rocks, or other natural objects. It was probably natural for Lowell to try to impose some sort of order on the barely visible details that could be seen on Mars. Once the idea of canals took hold, the sheer expectation of finding them led many people to see canals where there were none.

In 1903, in response to the debate surrounding the canals, British scientist E. Walter Maunder tried an experiment. He placed a drawing in front of a group of two hundred schoolboys arranged at different distances from it. He then asked them to sketch what they saw. The ones nearest the drawing drew it fairly accurately, but the ones farthest away drew lines very much like the canals Lowell saw.

This drawing is similar to the one used in Maunder's experiment.

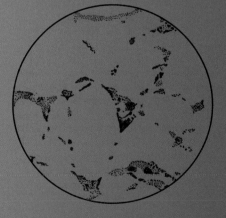

The monstrous Martian invaders from H. G. Wells's *The War of the Worlds* (1898) as depicted in one of the book's original illustrations

Today, Mars is still a popular subject for science fiction, though authors take a much more realistic approach. Kim Stanley Robinson's famous trilogy, *Red Mars* (1993), *Blue Mars* (1995), and *Green Mars* (1997), describes the exploration and future colonization of the planet with scrupulous attention to scientific detail and realism.

The truth about Mars, however, has turned out to be far stranger than any science fiction novel.

CHAPTER THREE

THE EXPLORATION OF MARS

Just about everything that could be learned about Mars from Earth-based instruments had been discovered by the early part of the twentieth century. Data were refined and measurements made more accurate, but little new information was attained.

One of the problems was that Mars could be observed only from the surface of Earth, which meant that astronomers had to look through Earth's atmosphere. The air, which is always moving, makes the images of stars and planets shimmer and wobble, like something seen at the bottom of a stream of moving water. Astronomers simply watched patiently for those rare moments of perfect visibility, when for a split second or so the atmosphere held still and Mars would suddenly stand out in razor-sharp detail.

Unfortunately, the only way to record these moments of perfect visibility was limited to the drawing skill of the individual astronomer—and not all astronomers were very good artists. Besides, such drawings—even those created by the most skillful observers   were subject to the biases and expectations of the astronomer (as in Percival Lowell's case).

FACTS ABOUT MARS

DIAMETER: 4,212 miles (6,779 km); about half that of Earth

MASS: 0.107 times that of Earth

SURFACE GRAVITY AT EQUATOR: 0.38 times that of Earth

LENGTH OF DAY: 24.6 hours

LENGTH OF YEAR: 686.979 Earth days, 668.599 Mars days

AVERAGE DISTANCE FROM SUN: 141,635,350 miles (227,940,000 km or 1.52 AU)

NUMBER OF MOONS: 2

The sizes of Earth, the Moon, and Mars to scale

Cameras, of course, could record pictures of the planets, but they required long exposures. Instead of being able to separate out those rare moments of clarity, cameras recorded the bad with the good and the longer an exposure took, the blurrier the photo became. No photo, however good, ever showed as much detail as the best drawing. This drove astronomers crazy—especially those who believed in the canals—because a photograph couldn't show that kind of fine detail. Astronomers didn't have anything that could prove the canals were real and not just optical illusions or figments of their imagination.

So during the opening decades of the twentieth century, research seemed to reach a stalemate. Frustrated astronomers had to put the study of Mars aside, and it didn't resume until the first spaceships could reach the planet.

The First Close-up Look

The whole world waited in eager anticipation for close-up pictures of the Martian canals as the *Mariner 4* spacecraft made the first-ever flyby of the planet in 1965. What would the probe reveal? A vast system of artificial canals? Ruined cities? An active civilization? When the pictures finally arrived, the disappointment was terrific.

Not only were there no canals, let alone lost cities, the planet looked just like the Moon! Instead of canals, there were just craters, craters, and more craters. Could Mars possibly be as dull as all that? Far from being the abode of life, as Lowell had described it and as so many had expected, Mars seemed totally dead.

The next two probes to reach Mars, *Mariners* 6 and 7, didn't reveal much more. The first sent back twenty-five close-up photos and the latter thirty-three. All of them showed a cratered Mars not much different from the one photographed by *Mariner 4*. But there were a few new discoveries. For instance, the craters looked more eroded than expected, and there appeared to be two distinct types of terrain: the floor of the Hellas basin, which appeared to be smooth and devoid of not only craters but just about any other sort of feature, and wild-looking, jumbled, broken landscapes that were like nothing on either Earth or the Moon. Still, Mars remained disappointing for all those who had looked forward to many surprises. It turned out, however, that the astronomers had been jumping to conclusions a little too quickly. Not until the next space probe, an orbiter called *Mariner 9*, reached Mars in 1971 did they find out just how badly they'd misjudged the red planet.

Mars, however, does not give up its secrets easily. Astronomers were looking forward to getting better pictures from the next space probe, but when they received the first photos from *Mariner 9* they were astonished to see . . . nothing at all! Mars looked like a blank, gray ball. The entire planet was covered in a worldwide dust storm that blanketed the surface from pole to pole. All they could do was wait.

One of the first of many amazing discoveries was made while the dust storm still covered Mars. Scientists noticed several dusky spots in the otherwise blank cloud cover. They realized that one of these coincided with an area that had been on Martian maps for a century. Schiaparelli had named it Nix Olympica, or "the snows of

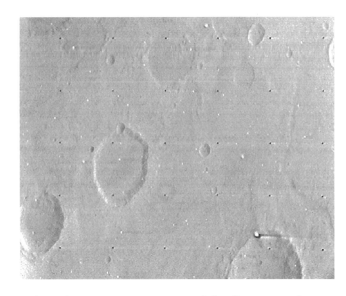

When the *Mariner 6* returned the first-ever close-up photos of Mars, most scientists were surprised —and perhaps a little disappointed—to see a cratered planet that looked not unlike Earth's moon. (The grid of black dots is created by the spacecraft's camera to allow astronomers to detect distortions in the photograph.) (NASA)

When *Mariner 9* arrived, the surface of Mars was hidden beneath a vast dust storm. Once the storm began to clear, scientists saw a dark spot that appeared above the receding dust (near the top of the photo). They did not know it at the time, but this is the peak of the largest volcano in the solar system. (NASA)

Olympus," because the dark spot was often brightened by a white patch that might have been either a frost deposit or clouds. Now Nix Olympica was suspected to be a vast mountain, higher than any other then known in the entire solar system—so high that its peak protruded though the pall of dust. Three other dark spots nearby were suspected of being huge mountains as well. Hints of craters in the centers of the spots suggested that all four mountains might even be enormous volcanoes.

The dust soon began to settle and, like a stage being revealed by a rising curtain, an amazing new Mars was slowly unveiled. One of the first wonders photographed was a vast canyon stretching nearly 1,900 miles (3,000 km) across the face of the planet. At places the canyon was 60 to 125 miles (100–200 km) wide and several miles deep. The Grand Canyon of Arizona would disappear within it.

Nix Olympica was finally revealed to be, in fact, an enormous volcano, higher than Earth's Mount Everest and covering more territory than the state of Nebraska! Once it was realized that Nix Olympica was a mountain, astronomers changed its name to Olympus **Mons**, or Mount Olympus.

With the dust gone, *Mariner 9* settled down to the business of mapping the entire globe. Every frame sent back to Earth seemed to show how wrong astronomers had been in thinking Mars was like the Moon. As it turned out, it couldn't possibly be more different. Photos showed fields of sand dunes, like those in the Sahara Desert, more huge volcanoes and canyons, and, perhaps the biggest surprise of all, meandering channels that looked more than anything else like ancient riverbeds.

Since *Mariner 9,* several other space probes have visited the planet. Of these, the most important have been the Viking, Pathfinder, Orbiter, and Mars Exploration Rovers missions. Other missions have included the European Space Agency's Mars Express, which consisted of an orbiter and a lander. The orbiter has worked perfectly, returning excellent images of the Martian surface along with other information, but the lander, unfortunately, failed.

The two Mars **rovers**, Spirit and Opportunity, which touched down on the red planet in January 2004, were sent specifically to search for signs of water—past or present—on Mars. They succeeded beyond all expectations. Not only have the rovers operated continuously for many months beyond their planned lifetime, they have found evidence that large amounts of water once flowed on Mars. This evidence is in the form of chemical alterations in many of the rocks that have been examined. For instance, certain forms of the mineral hematite were found that can only form in the presence of water.

Perhaps the rovers' most important discovery is that not only did water once flow in rivers and streams, but that it collected in large, shallow seas. Since these must have existed for thousands or perhaps even millions of years in order to produce the deposits the rovers found—including fossil ripple marks created by waves millions of years old—there may have been time for life to have formed in them.

For the future, NASA has plans for the *Mars Reconnaissance Orbiter,* which will search for water on the planet, and a Mars sample return mission that will bring specimens of Martian rocks and soil back to Earth.

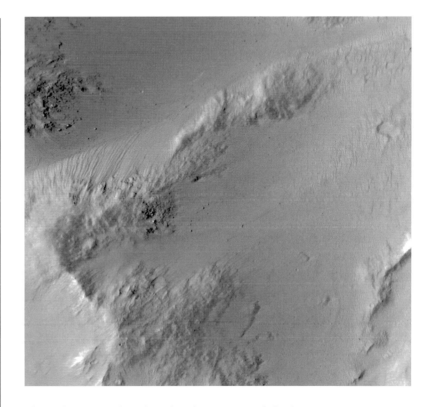

This photograph taken by the *Mars Global Surveyor* shows a typical Martian landscape: smooth dust-covered surfaces as well as bare, rocky surfaces. Small rounded knobs, such as those visible in the upper left corner, are boulders. A few of these have rolled down the slopes into the valleys. The area shown is only about 2 by 3 miles (3 by 5 km). (NASA/JPL /Malin Space Science Systems)

Two *Viking* landers set down on the surface of Mars in July 1976. Top: The area around the *Viking 1* landing site. (The gray object on the right is part of the spacecraft.) Bottom: A panoramic view from the *Viking 2* landing site. (NASA)

A rock called Half Dome was photographed from only a few feet away by the Sojourner rover. The hundreds of small pits are the result of bubbles forming in the rock when it was still molten. (NASA/JPL)

The Sojourner rover of the Mars Pathfinder mission examines a rock. The rover was designed to perform several different chemical and mineralogical tests on the rocks and soil, as well as to take photographs. (NASA/JPL)

Top: The Opportunity Mars rover captured this panoramic image of Endurance Crater in July 2004. The crater allowed scientists to see a rich cross section of the surface of Mars. Bottom left: Each layer of these rocks in Endurance Crater reveals a different period of Mars' history. The deeper the layer, the further back in time the rocks were formed. The rocks and the surfaces between them are covered by small, round, dark pebbles that may have formed within a body of water. Bottom right: An approximate true-color image taken by the Mars Exploration rover Spirit shows a view of the peaklike outcrop atop "West Spur," part of the Columbia Hills that the rover later explored. (NASA/JPL)

There are several types of robot space explorers, or *probes*. An *orbiter* does not land on a planet but instead remains in orbit around it. A *lander* sets down on the surface, while a *rover* is a wheeled vehicle capable of roaming the surface. Of the more than thirty probes sent to Mars over the past forty years, more than two thirds have failed for one reason or another. Here is a list of the missions that made it:

NAME	NATIONALITY	LAUNCH	ARRIVAL	MAJOR ACCOMPLISHMENTS
Mariner 4	U.S.A.	11/28/64	7/14/65	Sent back 22 close-up photos and other information
Mariner 6	U.S.A.	2/25/69	7/31/69	Sent back 75 photos
Mariner 7	U.S.A.	3/27/69	8/5/69	Sent back 126 photos
Mars 2	U.S.S.R.	5/19/71	11/27/71	No orbiter photos because of dust storm. Lander failed.
Mariner 9	U.S.A.	5/30/71	11/14/71	Sent back photos of Phobos and Deimos, and 7,329 photos of Mars
Mars 4	U.S.S.R.	7/21/73	2/10/74	Sent back photos
Mars 5	U.S.S.R.	7/25/73	2/12/74	Sent back 70 photos
Viking 1	U.S.A.	8/20/75	6/19/76	Orbiter/lander mission—first photos of Mars's surface
Viking 2	U.S.A.	9/9/75	8/7/76	Orbiter/lander mission—the two *Vikings* sent back more than 50,000 photos
Mars Global Surveyor	U.S.A.	11/7/96	9/11/97	Detailed survey and mapping of the entire planet
Mars Pathfinder	U.S.A.	12/4/96	7/4/97	Landed the first rover, Sojourner
Mars Express	European Space Agency	6/2/03	12/25/03	Orbiter (an attached lander failed)
Mars Exploration Rovers	U.S.A.	5/30/03 6/25/03	1/04	Two spacecraft, each carrying a lander and a rover

CHAPTER FOUR

THE BIOGRAPHY OF A PLANET

The currently accepted theory of the evolution of the solar system suggests that the Sun and planets formed about 4.5 billion years ago from an enormous cloud of dust and gas. The cloud was large enough for the gravitation of its individual particles to start the cloud contracting and to keep the contraction going. But once this process began, the cloud must have shrunk to a millionth of its original size very quickly. During this collapse it became what is known as a **protostar**.

As more and more particles gathered in the center of the cloud, it became denser, and as it became denser its gravity increased. This, in turn, caused it to collapse even further. Soon this core began to heat up (for much the same reason that the air in a bicycle pump grows warmer as you compress it), glowing red within the dark cloud. The intense heat and pressure caused a nuclear reaction to begin—perhaps only a few thousand years after the cloud first began to condense. As soon as this happened, the protostar, in which no nuclear reactions can take place, became a star, which is powered by nuclear reactions.

The increased amount of heat this produced created an outward pressure that resisted the collapsing dust and gas . . . and the collapse came to a halt. The Hubble Space Telescope has observed possible young solar systems in just this phase of development. Called **protoplanetary disks**, they look like dark, bun-shaped disks, often with a dimly glowing center.

Meanwhile, within the cloud, tiny particles of dust collided and stuck together, forming tiny clumps of material. As these clumps—called **planetesimals**—grew in size, they attracted more and more particles. This process is called **accretion**. Most of the early collisions were relatively gentle, so the planetesimals didn't knock themselves into pieces. Eventually, grains of dust grew to the size of rocks, then boulders, and then asteroids miles across. The whole process of growing from the size of a large pinhead to a mountain may have taken only 100,000 years or so.

By this point the process began to slow down—the original dust and gas was being used up and the cloud grew thin. Several stars have been observed with large, thin disks of dust surrounding them—such as Beta Pictoris—which may be solar systems in this same stage of development.

As the planetesimals grew larger, their gravity increased and they began to move faster. The collisions between them became more violent. Instead of accreting, however, some of them shattered into pieces. The few planetesimals that were large enough to survive the collisions grew even larger, devouring the debris from the smaller objects. Once the process of accretion began, the planetesimals grew very quickly. In just a few tens of millions of years,

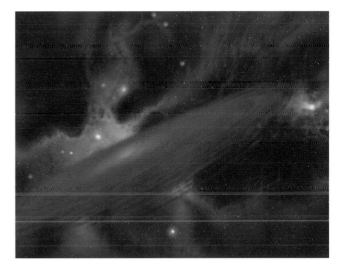

As the primordial cloud of dust and gas collapsed under its own gravity, the cloud began to rotate and flatten. The center began to glow as it grew denser.

As soon as the early Sun became dense enough and hot enough, fusion was triggered and a star was born.

these bodies grew from a cloud of dust and gas into the planets of our solar system.

During the period when Mars was accreting, the temperature of the planet was quite high. Mars started differentiating, which means that heavier molecules—such as iron and nickel—sank toward the center while the lighter substances were left near the surface. In this way, the present-day nickel-iron core was created. But because of the small size and gravity of Mars, the **differentiation** wasn't as thorough as it was on bigger planets, such as Earth or Venus. The **mantle** and the crust retained many heavy substances, such as iron and other metals, resulting in a relatively thick and inflexible solid crust. This means that the hot **magma** of the mantle has a hard time making its way to the surface. Therefore, volcanism and **plate tectonics** did not play as important a role in restructuring the surface of Mars as they would have on a planet with a thinner solid crust layer, such as Earth.

The thick, rigid crust of Mars prevented the formation of moving continental plates such as those on Earth (though in the distant past, Mars may have made a brief attempt at plate tectonics, when the vast canyon system of **Valles** Marineris was formed). This resulted in hot spots where volcanic activity occurred in one place over a very long time. The best evidence for this is the Tharsis region, which has several large **shield volcanoes**—the biggest in the solar system. A shield volcano is created by many flows of lava building up layer after layer over very long periods of time. The extreme height of the volcanoes of Mars shows how thick the crust must be: A thinner crust couldn't support the weight of the enormous mountains. The size of the

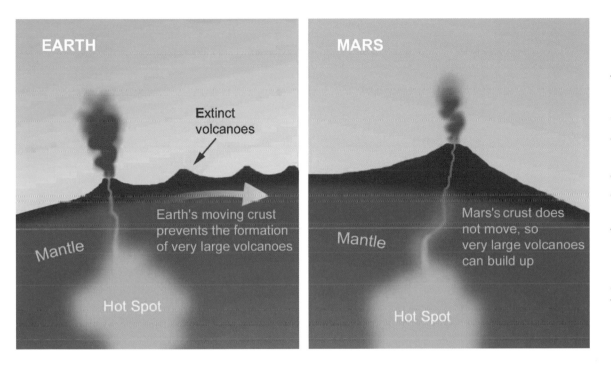

EARTH

MARS

Extinct volcanoes

Earth's moving crust prevents the formation of very large volcanoes

Mantle

Hot Spot

Mars's crust does not move, so very large volcanoes can build up

Mantle

Hot Spot

The moving plates of Earth's crust prevent giant volcanoes from forming. On Earth (left), as the crust moves over a hot spot in the mantle, the volcano that forms above it will eventually become extinct, with a new volcano forming farther down the line. In this way, chains of volcanoes will form, such as the Hawaiian Islands. On Mars (right), there are no moving crustal plates. When a volcano forms above a hot spot, it will just keep growing larger and larger.

volcanoes indicates that the activity that created them continued for an extremely long time.

In addition to the Tharsis area, there are many smaller volcanoes on Mars, most of which are located in the northern hemisphere, while the southern hemisphere is virtually untouched by major volcanism. This is one of the many mysteries of Mars that scientists hope future exploration will solve, but the result is that Mars is "two-faced." On one hand, there are southern highlands with heavy cratering that resemble the surface of the Moon.

Not very long ago there were a great many active volcanoes on the planet. Is there still volcanic activity on Mars? No one knows, though it is possible.

These are the oldest surface structures of the planet, possibly as old as 4 billion years. On the other hand, the volcanic activity in the north resulted in the plains of the northern lowlands, where the great volcanoes covered the early craters with lava. Therefore, the surface of the northern plains is newer than the southern highlands.

The volcanoes on Mars now appear to be pretty quiet—volcanic activity seems to have hit a peak around 3.3 billion years ago. While there is no evidence to suggest current volcanic activity, there is, on the other hand, no reason to think that all volcanism is extinct. The youngest lava flows from the Tharsis Montes have been dated between 2.5 billion and 0.1 billion years ago. (One of the ways by which astronomers can date lava flows is by counting the meteor craters in them. Younger flows have fewer craters.) However, some of the flows on Olympus Mons and among the northern lava plains have been dated to less than 100 million years, so it is not impossible that some volcanic activity may still be taking place.

CHAPTER FIVE

A MARTIAN WEATHER REPORT

Today will be warm and sunny with an average temperature expected around −76°F (−60°C) and an afternoon high of 68°F (20°C). Tonight's low at the poles will be −184°F (−120°C). No precipitation expected for the next several million years. Occasional dust storms.

This would be the typical morning weather forecast on Mars. It is a cold, dry desert world. It hasn't rained in millions of years. In fact, pure liquid water can't even exist on the open surface. If you were to pour a glassful onto the ground, it would just boil away until it was gone. An ice cube would merely disappear gradually. This is because the air pressure on Mars is so low. It is the heavy atmosphere on Earth that allows oceans, rivers, and lakes to exist.

The weight of air requires water to be raised to a high temperature—212°F (100°C) at sea level—before water will boil and turn into a gas. But as air pressure is lowered, the temperature needed to boil water is lowered as well. This is why it is difficult for people living at high altitudes to cook many foods—their

The *Viking* lander took this photo of Mars's early morning frost—the pale pinkish areas among the rocks. (NASA/JPL)

water starts boiling long before it reaches a high enough temperature for foods to cook properly. (If you were to go to a high enough altitude, the temperature of your body would be enough to make your blood boil!) If air pressure is lowered enough, the heat contained in the water itself would be enough to make it boil. The air pressure on Mars is so low that if water is warm enough to be liquid (instead of ice), it is warm enough to start boiling, so any pure liquid water on the surface of Mars will turn to vapor right away and disappear.

As long as it stays cold enough, however, water can exist as solid ice on the surface of Mars. The polar regions certainly fit this description. There are large masses of water ice permanently frozen at the poles. Also, there are almost certainly vast quantities of ice buried beneath the surface all over the planet, where the overlying rock and sand protects it from sunlight.

But just because Mars is cold and dry doesn't mean it has no weather. In fact, Mars has a very complex, active weather system. A typical day on Mars might be beautiful and clear, without a cloud in the bright pink sky and only a few wisps of dust raised by a slight breeze. It may be 40°F (4°C) with highs reaching 68°F (20°C). A few days later, however, the temperature might plummet 40 degrees or more with brilliant water ice clouds appearing in the sky. Then the following week a dust storm might blanket the entire planet under an opaque yellow cloud. Changes this dramatic can happen every week on Mars, with the planet experiencing abrupt planet-wide swings from dusty and hot to cloudy and cold. These shifts in climate are driven by three important factors: the thin

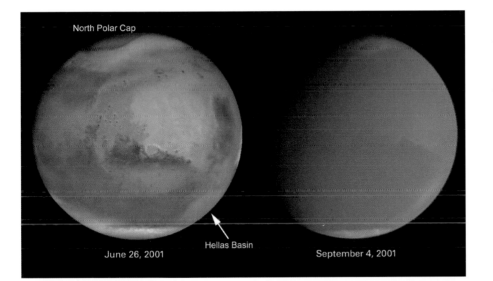

North Polar Cap

Hellas Basin

June 26, 2001

September 4, 2001

Left: These two photographs taken by the Hubble Space Telescope show a global dust storm that engulfed Mars at the beginning of Martian spring in the southern hemisphere. In June, the storm was just beginning in the Hellas Basin, with another storm starting at the northern polar cap. By early September, the dust raised by the storm obscured the surface features on the planet. This fine dust blocks a significant amount of sunlight from reaching the surface. This was the biggest storm seen in the past several decades. (NASA)

Below: Early morning mist fills the canyons of Noctis Labyrinthus—a vast complex of intersecting channels at the western end of Valles Marineris. (NASA/JPL/Malin Space Science Systems)

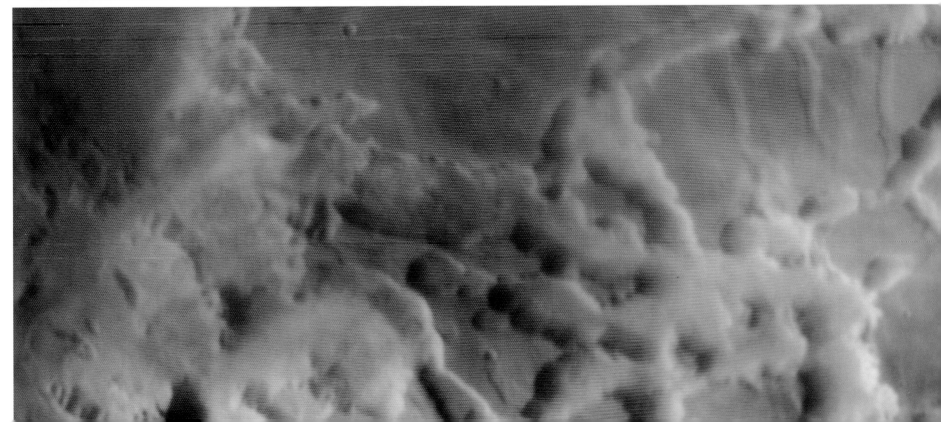

Dust devils like those in the distance stir up the talcum-fine dust, raising it high into the thin atmosphere.

atmosphere of Mars, its **elliptical** orbit around the Sun, and the effects of dust and water ice clouds in the atmosphere.

Extreme Climate

As we've already seen, Mars has a very thin atmosphere. Earth's atmosphere is a hundred times denser than that of Mars. In fact, the atmosphere of Mars is as thin as Earth's atmosphere at an altitude of nearly 22 miles (35 km). Because the atmosphere of Mars is so thin and because there are no oceans to store up heat from the Sun, the temperature of the planet responds more quickly and intensely to surface changes and atmospheric heating.

The Sun heats Mars's surface rapidly, which in turn warms the air above, causing it to rise. As warm air rises and cold air sinks, winds are generated. Since most of Mars's surface is covered with dust as fine as the particles in cigarette smoke, even weak winds can easily stir it up. Tornado-like dust devils—small whirlwinds—occur during the day when the heated air rises rapidly and becomes turbulent. Scientists believe that these dust devils are the primary force for getting dust high up into the air. When the prevailing winds become strong, they can cause violent regional storms.

Even though Mars's atmosphere is thin, its winds can still reach surprising velocities. While wind speeds measured at the two *Viking* lander sites were usually a gentle 10 miles per hour (16 km/h) or less, there were gusts of up to 30 miles per hour (48 km/h). At the height of a major dust storm, however, winds may reach hundreds of miles an hour.

A day on Mars is almost exactly as long as a day on Earth, and the axis of Mars is tipped almost the same, so Mars has seasons very similar to our own—winter, spring, summer, and fall. A year on Mars, however, is almost twice as long as a year on Earth, so its seasons are also twice as long. This has an effect on Mars's climate, but the most important factors in the climate involve the distance of Mars from the Sun and the shape of its orbit.

Mars is half again farther from the Sun than Earth is. The Sun appears only two thirds the size it does in Earth's sky, so it seems 2.25 times dimmer and provides 2.25 times less heat than it does for our planet. This makes Mars a colder planet. But the most important effect is caused by the shape of Mars's orbit.

All of the planets travel around the Sun in elliptical orbits. The orbit of Earth is so close to a circle that the varying distance from the Sun is very slight. The difference between the closest and farthest distances from the Sun in Earth's orbit is only 4 million miles (6.4 million km), a 4 percent difference. This has hardly any effect on Earth's climate. Mars, however, has a very elliptical orbit. It swings 25 million miles (40 million km) closer to the Sun when it is nearest than when it is farthest away, a 20 percent difference. This has a very noticeable effect on Mars's climate, leading to planet-wide changes in atmospheric and surface temperatures over the course of a Martian year.

During **perihelion**, when Mars is at its closest approach to the Sun (and it is summer in its southern hemisphere), the planet receives 40 percent more sunlight than during **aphelion**, when it is farthest from the Sun (and it is summer in its northern hemisphere).

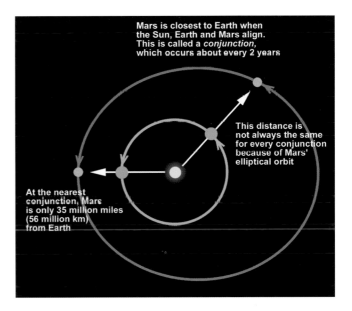

Mars is closest to Earth when the Sun, Earth and Mars align. This is called a *conjunction*, which occurs about every 2 years

This distance is not always the same for every conjunction because of Mars' elliptical orbit

At the nearest conjunction, Mars is only 35 million miles (56 million km) from Earth

Every time Mars, Earth, and the Sun line up, Earth and Mars make a close approach to each other. Because the orbit of Mars is much more elliptical than Earth's, however, this distance can be as close as 35 million miles (56,327,000 km) and as far away as 62 million miles (99,780,000 km).

Moreover, Mars's southern hemisphere is tilted toward the Sun when the planet's elliptical orbit swings it closest to the Sun, and its northern hemisphere is tilted toward the Sun when Mars is farthest from the Sun. As a result, the southern summer is considerably hotter than the northern summer. This extra heat pouring into the southern hemisphere increases the circulation of the atmosphere and drives stronger winds.

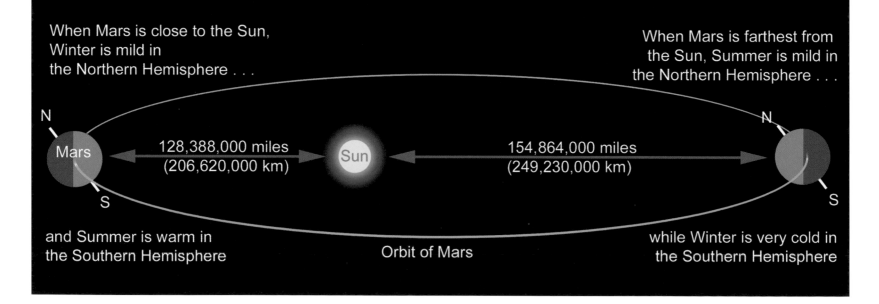

The changing distance of Mars from the Sun during the course of a year affects the severity of its seasons . . .

When Mars is close to the Sun, Winter is mild in the Northern Hemisphere . . .

When Mars is farthest from the Sun, Summer is mild in the Northern Hemisphere . . .

N

Mars

128,388,000 miles (206,620,000 km)

Sun

154,864,000 miles (249,230,000 km)

N

S

S

and Summer is warm in the Southern Hemisphere

Orbit of Mars

while Winter is very cold in the Southern Hemisphere

The large disparity in temperature between the two hemispheres helps generate the winds that create continental-scale dust storms. The dust may be swept to altitudes of tens of miles, where it spreads globally. Then the dust cloud absorbs even more heat from the Sun, causing the atmosphere to further warm up.

The climate changes drastically when Mars is farthest from the Sun. Wide belts of water-ice clouds form instead of planet-wide dust storms as water vapor in the atmosphere crystallizes. Surface dust raised by the relatively milder winds of winter is eventually removed from the atmosphere as ice crystals surround the dust particles and carry them to the ground. Without dust in the air to absorb sunlight, the air grows even colder. This competition between heating from dust and cooling by clouds drives large-scale annual and short-term changes in Mars's regional climates.

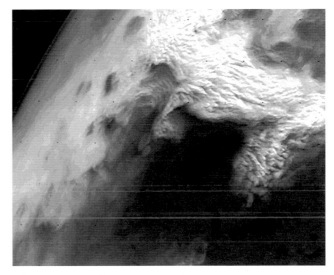

This *Viking* orbiter image shows a large storm on Mars that soon grew into a global dust storm. (NASA/JPL)

Vast dust storms form on Mars and
can blanket thousands of square miles
and sometimes even the entire planet.

OBSERVING MARS THROUGH A TELESCOPE

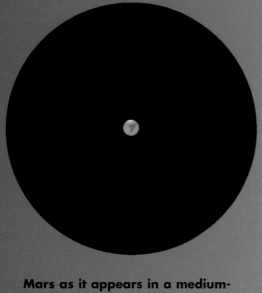

Mars as it appears in a medium-sized telescope

Although Mars can easily be seen with even a small telescope, one of the problems for the amateur observer is that it is not a very large planet—only about twice the size of the Moon. Every 26 months or so, Earth catches up with Mars and overtakes it. When this happens, the two planets come close together. Because their orbits are elliptical, this distance can range from 0.38 to 0.68 astronomical units (AU). Although this is closer to Earth than any planet other than Venus, even when it is at its closest approach to Earth, Mars is still nearly 35 million miles (55.7 million km) away—140 times farther away than the Moon. Even through a large 40-inch (100-cm) telescope, Mars appears about 0.1 inch (0.25 cm) wide.

What makes Mars exciting to view, even in a small telescope, is that it is the only planet whose surface features are clearly visible from Earth. The white spot of one of the polar caps will probably stand out, as well as perhaps one of the more prominent dark areas. At first, though, Mars may be a disappointing sight, even in a large telescope. However, with practice, a lot more detail will become visible. Perhaps you will see one of the great dust storms that sometimes blank out a large section of the surface or even the entire planet.

It would be worth having a pencil and paper available so you can sketch some of the markings you may see. It will make things easier if you have some circles already drawn on the paper—2-inch circles would be a good size. Having one of the many maps of Mars nearby will help you identify any features you may see. The moons of Mars, however, are visible only through the very largest telescopes. Astronomy magazines and some of the Web sites listed at the end of this book will tell you where to find Mars in the night sky.

CHAPTER SIX

BLUE MARS?

Although Mars is a cold, dry planet today, it probably hasn't always been so. The evidence for freely flowing water in Mars's early history is dramatic. The southern highlands are crisscrossed by networks of valleys that appear to have been formed by water. And many craters are surrounded by a ring of splattered debris, like that around a stone dropped in soft mud.

The idea that Mars could have had water astonished most astronomers. As we have seen, Mars is a small planet with a very thin atmosphere. Any pure liquid water on the surface would quickly evaporate, and the molecules would eventually disappear into space, lost forever. Yet, not only does Mars boast the largest volcanoes and deepest canyons in the solar system, it also shows evidence for the most catastrophic floods.

Large channels, which could have been formed only by the massive release of water over a short period of time, scar four regions—Chryse Planitia, Elysium Planitia, the eastern Hellas Basin, and the Amazonis Planitia (see map page 49). Several of these channels drain into the northern plains, lending support to a theory that an ancient ocean may have once covered most of the northern hemisphere.

These are some of the mesas and mounds found within Valles Marineris. The layers that are visible may be deposits from ancient lakes and shallow seas; however, some scientists believe that these layers are simply deposits of airborne dust that were later buried and cemented to create cliff-forming rock. Each layer is about the same thickness, estimated to be about 33 feet (10 m). (NASA/JPL/Malin Space Science Systems)

The impact that created this crater appears to have melted underground ice, which "splashed" liquefied soil over the surrounding landscape like a stone thrown into mud. (NASA/JPL)

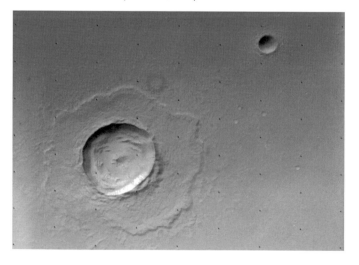

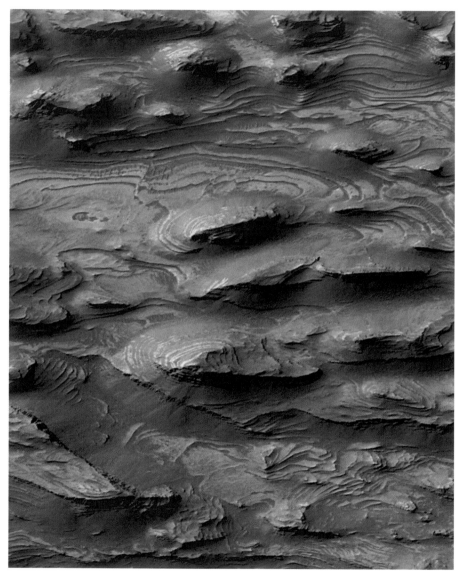

This is what Mars's historic floods might have looked like. Underground ice exposed in the face of the distant cliffs is melting, creating a rushing river of water that is eroding a deep channel.

These outflow channels can be truly enormous. Typically, they are a few tens of miles across at their source, expanding downstream to hundreds of miles across. Discharge rates have been estimated at 10,000 times the average discharge of Earth's largest rivers, such as the Mississippi.

Some of the Martian floods appear to have been 100 times larger than the biggest flood known on Earth. This occurred in the state of Washington about 10,000 years ago, when an ice dam burst, releasing a 1,000-foot (300-m) wall of water flowing at 386 million cubic feet (11 million m^3) per second, or about ten times the combined flow of all the rivers on Earth. The land downstream from this flood—now called the Scablands—has the same features that appear downstream in the Martian channels.

The formation of these large channels didn't require a steady supply of liquid water. They needed only a source of underground ice. Some outflow channels, such as those to the east of the Valles Marineris, seem to have occurred, like the flood in the Scablands, when an ice dam suddenly collapsed. But others emerge from regions where the ground seems to have collapsed, leaving a chaotic jumble of large blocks of rock. There are similar areas of **chaotic terrain** on Earth in Siberia. They formed when a layer of underground ice melted suddenly, causing the rock above to fracture and collapse. On Earth, this melting was almost always caused by climatic changes, but on Mars the ice could have been melted by the heat of a nearby asteroid impact.

Some of the Martian meteorites that have been found on Earth also support the idea of a wet Mars. One meteorite in particular is made of minerals that were dated from 1.3 billion years ago.

Facing page: The rippled floor of an ancient flood channel is all that remains of the vast flood that once poured through the land millions of years ago. Scientists hope that fossils might someday be discovered buried beneath ancient riverbeds such as this.

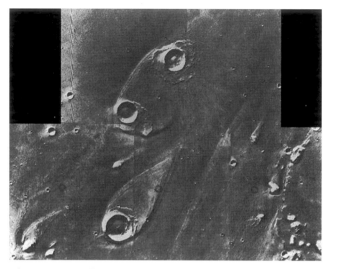

These streamlined, teardrop-shaped islands were among the earliest evidence found that water once flowed on Mars. As the flood streamed from the lower left to the upper right, it cut the channels and eroded the land around the craters. (There was no photographic data available for the black boxes in the corners.) (NASA/JPL)

The meteorite was exposed to water, however, as recently as 670 million years ago, long before it was blasted off the surface of Mars by the impact of an asteroid. It may have been only a trace of water, but it was enough to alter the minerals of which the rock was made.

Where Did It Go?

Scientists think that liquid water must have existed on the surface of Mars before 3.8 billion years ago. Many of the features on Mars that were created by water could only have formed if the water was able to remain exposed on the surface for long periods of time. But the atmosphere on Mars today is too cold to support liquid water on the surface for long, and too thin in most areas for water ice to form—it would quickly **sublimate** directly into water vapor. This suggests that Mars used to be much warmer and wetter than it is today.

If Mars once had so much water, where did it go? A large amount may have been lost to space, but scientists believe that much of the water might still remain on Mars in the form of underground ice lying not far beneath the surface. This would be similar to the permanent layer of ice—the permafrost—that lies beneath the tundra of Alaska and Canada. At the equator, for instance, the top of the ice layer on Mars may be between 1,000 and 3,000 feet (300 to 910 m) beneath the surface, where the ice may be as thick as 0.6 to 1.9 miles (1 to 3 km). At higher latitudes, it may be only 500 to 1,000 feet (150 to 300 m) beneath the surface and 1.9 to 4.3 miles (3 to 7 km) thick.

In 2002 the *Mars Global Surveyor* spacecraft detected signs of hydrogen atoms that suggest the presence of what may be a vast "ocean" of underground ice. Images from the orbiter have also revealed channels or gullies that may be evidence of groundwater seeping from the slopes of craters and valleys in the southern hemisphere. Since this seepage occurs on *top* of sand dunes, the channels and gullies must have been created more recently than the dunes. It's possible that the dunes may be millions of years old, but if they are in an area where dunes are constantly changing and being re-created, the water deposits may be very young.

Some scientists have concluded that water is still flowing on Mars. The reason this is possible on a planet where liquid water cannot exist for long in the open air is that this water is probably brine—water with a lot of mineral salts dissolved in it. This would keep the water from evaporating so quickly.

CHAPTER SEVEN

A TOUR OF MARS

There are several distinct regions of special interest on Mars: the giant volcanoes, the great canyon systems, the channels and valleys, the deserts and dunes, and the polar caps.

Volcanoes

More than half the surface of Mars shows the effects of volcanism. There are either huge volcanic mountains or vast lava plains covering thousands of square miles. The most prominent area is called Tharsis. This region is a vast bulge 2,485 miles (4,000 km) wide that rises 6 miles (10 km) high at its center. It is so large that it actually affects the rotation of the planet, in the same way adding a weight to the rim of a rotating wheel will make it wobble.

Topping the Tharsis bulge is a collection of volcanoes greater than any known in the rest of the solar system. Three of these line up in a row down the center of Tharsis: Arsia Mons, Pavonis Mons, and Ascraeus Mons. Each of them is larger than any volcano on Earth.

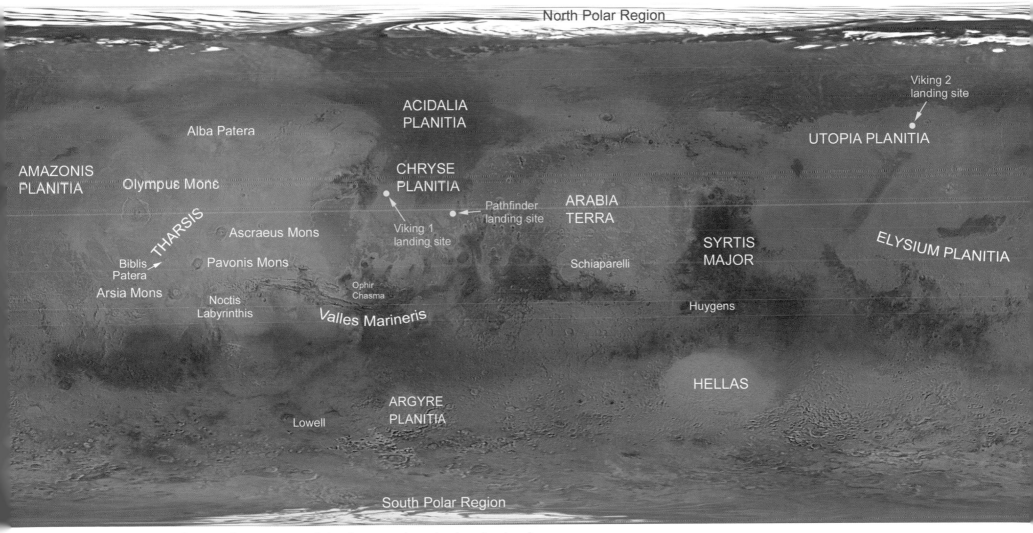

North Polar Region

ACIDALIA PLANITIA

Alba Patera

CHRYSE PLANITIA

AMAZONIS PLANITIA

Olympus Mons

ARABIA TERRA

Pathfinder landing site

Viking 1 landing site

THARSIS

Ascraeus Mons

SYRTIS MAJOR

Biblis Patera

Pavonis Mons

Schiaparelli

Arsia Mons

Ophir Chasma

Noctis Labyrinthis

Valles Marineris

Huygens

Viking 2 landing site

UTOPIA PLANITIA

ELYSIUM PLANITIA

HELLAS

ARGYRE PLANITIA

Lowell

South Polar Region

This map of Mars shows many of the features described in this book.

This is Biblis Patera, a small shield volcano located between Olympus Mons and Arsia Mons. The volcano is 109 by 65 miles (175 by 105 km), and the caldera at the summit is 31 miles (50 km) across. The slopes of the mountain are cut by long, straight fractures. (NASA/JPL)

Just north of Tharsis lies Alba **Patera**, a volcanic feature more than 932 miles (1,500 km) wide—more than ten times wider than Hawaii's Mauna Loa, Earth's largest volcano. Alba Patera is a very strange feature, unlike anything else in the solar system. Although it is huge, it is nearly flat, rising scarcely 2 miles (3.2 km) above the surrounding terrain.

The reason for the enormous size of the Tharsis volcanoes is the lack of moving plates of surface crust, such as Earth has (see diagram page 29). Most volcanoes occur above "hot spots" deep beneath the surface of the planet. These hot spots stay in one place while the surface crust moves above them. This means that a volcano will remain active only so long as it stays above its hot spot. If the crust moves the volcano away, it will die, like a pan of boiling water moved away from its burner. The chain of volcanoes that forms the Hawaiian Islands is a result of the crust moving over a single hot spot. Currently, the island of Hawaii is over the hot spot, and its volcano, Mauna Kea, is active. Sometime in the future, however, it will move away and gradually die, joining the other extinct volcanoes in the island chain, while an entirely new volcano will erupt to take its place.

The volcanoes on Mars, however, tend to sit on top of their hot spots forever. This means that lava and ash will just keep pouring out, building up layer after layer, with the volcano getting bigger and higher with every eruption.

The greatest of the volcanoes is Olympus Mons. Dwarfing even the huge volcanoes of the Tharsis bulge, it has fifteen times the mass of Mauna Loa. Olympus Mons sits to the northwest of the main Tharsis area and towers 15 miles (24 km) above the sur-

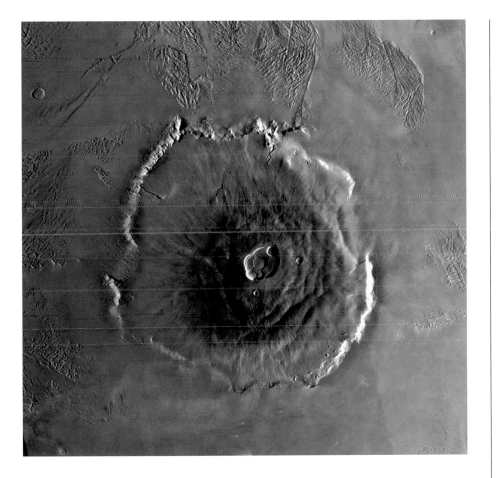

Left: The giant volcano Olympus Mons as seen from orbit (NASA/JPL)

Below: A close-up view of the **caldera** of Olympus Mons: A caldera is a large crater formed by collapse rather than by impact or explosion. The caldera of Olympus Mons is as large as Yellowstone National Park. Several smaller calderas are also visible within the larger one. Two impact craters that were caused by meteorites are outside the caldera, around the edge of the photo. (NASA/JPL/Malin Space Science Systems)

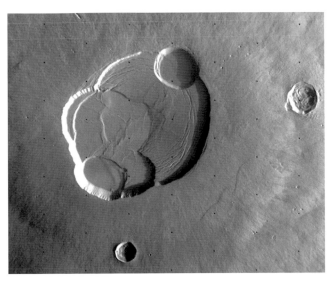

rounding landscape. It is three times as high as Mount Everest—Earth's tallest mountain—is above sea level. The base of Olympus Mons would entirely cover the state of Missouri. Bright patches that had been observed since the nineteenth century turned out to be high clouds that often form above the lofty mountain.

A view across a typical volcanic caldera on Mars: The relatively flat floor of the vast crater features several smaller calderas and two or three small cinder cones. Although scientists don't know if Martian volcanoes are still active, the fresh sulfur deposits around the vent in the foreground might indicate recent activity.

Olympus Mons and its neighboring volcanoes are relatively young, less than 3 billion years old. Although there is no evidence to suggest that any of these volcanoes are still active, neither is there any reason to suspect that volcanic activity on Mars is entirely extinct. There may still be enough heat beneath the surface to melt water and create occasional springs.

Canyons

Just to the east of Tharsis is the system of canyons called Valles Marineris, or Mariner valleys, named after the *Mariner 9* spacecraft that discovered it. The canyon system begins near the middle of the Tharsis bulge as a complex of intertwining canyons and valleys called Noctis Labyrinthus—"Labyrinth of the Night." The system merges to the east into the greatest canyon known in the solar system. While Earth's Grand Canyon stretches across the northwestern corner of Arizona for 280 miles (450 km), Valles Marineris would stretch across the United States from the Atlantic Ocean to the Pacific Ocean. With a depth of up to 3 to 4 miles (5 to 7 km), it is about four times deeper than the Grand Canyon. Valles Marineris is so long that when one end has moved well into night, the other end is still in daylight. The difference in temperature this could cause might result in powerful winds tearing down the length of the canyon.

It is not really fair, however, to compare Valles Marineris to the Grand Canyon. It has not been carved out by water, as the Grand Canyon was on Earth. It is actually the result of enormous blocks of the Martian crust moving apart during a brief period of tectonic activity many millions of years in the past.

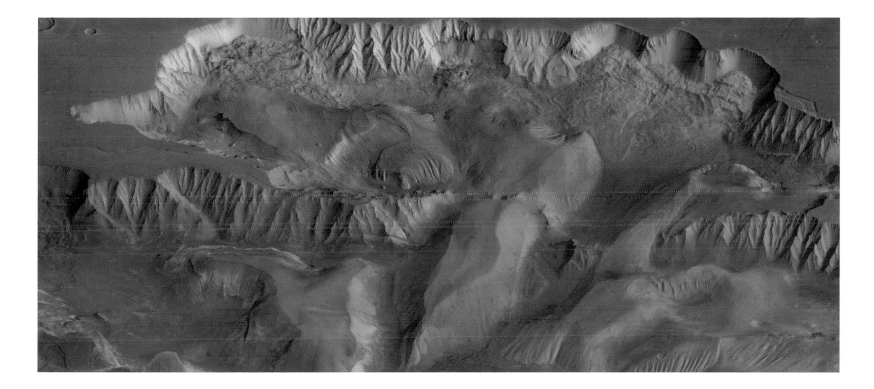

It would be much more accurate to compare Valles Marineris to features on Earth such as the Red Sea, the Great Rift Valley of Africa, or—perhaps best of all—the Atlantic Ocean. These are all features that are being created by the crust of our planet pulling apart. In fact, Valles Marineris may look as the Atlantic Ocean did more than 100 million years ago, when the Americas first began to pull away from Europe and Africa.

Valles Marineris also has a central ridge like the Atlantic Ocean, which has the Midatlantic Ridge running down its center.

A view of central Valles Marineris: The area near the top of the image is Ophir Chasma, which is approximately 186 miles (300 km) wide and as deep as 6.2 miles (10 km). The interconnected valleys of Valles Marineris may have formed from a combination of erosion and tectonic activity. Numerous landslides are visible in the canyon walls. (NASA/JPL)

(53)

Coprates is a vast canyon in the eastern half of the great Valles Marineris system.

This is caused by the upwelling of fresh material from the mantle as the crust is pulled apart. However, while the Atlantic Ocean continues to widen, the forces that created Valles Marineris stopped millions of years ago.

Much of the present-day Valles Marineris has been shaped by forces other than movement of the crust. Since it was originally formed, erosion—perhaps by water—and landslides have sculpted a great deal of the vast canyon.

Channels and Valleys

To the north and east of Valles Marineris are vast regions of large flood channels. Most of these emerge from areas of chaotic terrain. Chaotic terrains are areas where the surface has been broken up into a jumbled, confused mass of broken blocks. They are lower than the surrounding plains and are encircled by cliffs. Chaotic terrains seem to have been the result of ice melting beneath the surface. When the water ran off, the surface above collapsed. Large flood channels emerge from these areas, extending and converging for thousands of miles on the plains of Chryse Planitia.

Many of these channels appear to be the result of catastrophic flooding, like that which created the Washington Scablands on Earth. Others are more riverlike, and may have been created by slower-moving streams that existed for thousands and even millions of years.

Deserts and Dunes

Mars is a desert world, and nothing is a better reminder of this than the vast regions covered with dust and wind-blown dunes.

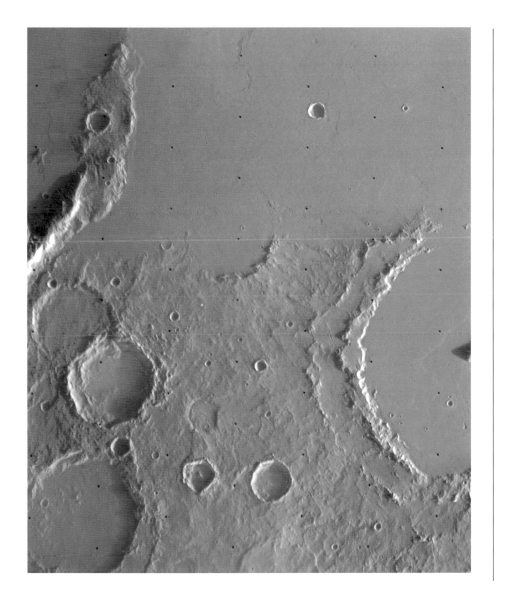

The most striking feature of Mars is its red color. Even when seen with the naked eye, Mars appears to be bright red. In photos taken from the surface of Mars, *everything* about Mars is red. The rocks are red, the sand dunes are red, even the sky is salmon pink. But *why* is Mars red?

The soil on Mars consists of clays that contain large amounts of iron-rich minerals. This iron has combined with oxygen to form iron oxides, which are a reddish color. If you have ever seen a rusty piece of iron or steel, you have seen iron oxide. Mars is red because it is rusting.

These craters are almost completely buried beneath drifting sand. (NASA/JPL/Malin Space Science Systems)

(57)

Much of Mars is covered with thousands of square miles of deserts and sand dunes.

Dust is everywhere on Mars. It fills craters like water fills potholes; it flows into valleys and covers rocks. It even fills the air so that the sky is colored a soft pink.

Mars is the only planet other than Earth that is known to have features sculpted by wind. The constant winds sandblast rocks, mountains, valleys, and craters. Ever-changing dune fields surround the poles and cover vast plains. A sea of sand larger than any similar area on Earth covers more than 1 million square miles (5 million km^2) and encircles the north pole.

The Polar Caps

The polar caps were among the first features to be observed on Mars, and astronomers were certain from the very beginning that they were either frozen water or frozen carbon dioxide (what we are familiar with as "dry ice"), or a combination of both. Today we know that each polar cap has a permanent, residual layer of water ice that is covered by a larger, seasonal cap of carbon dioxide ice.

The north and south polar caps are not identical. This is because the climate of the northern hemisphere is not the same as that of the southern. Mars's axial tilt creates seasons. When the northern hemisphere is tilted toward the Sun, for instance, it is summer there and winter in the southern hemisphere. Six months later, the northern hemisphere is tilted away from the Sun and the seasons are reversed. Earth has an almost perfectly circular orbit, so the seasons in the northern hemisphere are not very different from the seasons in the southern hemisphere. The orbit of Mars, on the other hand,

This view from the *Viking* orbiter shows an area where there was once a large deposit of underground ice. When the ice melted, the landscape above it collapsed, and the escaping water cut the channel that runs off toward the left. (NASA/JPL)

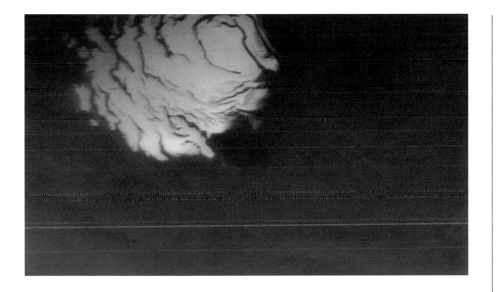

This is the south polar cap of Mars as photographed by the *Mars Global Surveyor*. In winter and early spring, this entire scene would be covered by frost. In summer, the cap shrinks to its minimum size, as shown here. The polar cap from left to right is about 260 miles (420 km) across. (NASA/JPL/Malin Space Science Systems)

is elliptical. When it is summer in the southern hemisphere, Mars is closest to the Sun, but when it is summer in the northern hemisphere, Mars is farthest from the Sun. This means that summers are much warmer in the south than in the north.

When Mars is nearest the Sun, the increased solar radiation creates a large temperature difference between the lower and upper parts of the atmosphere. This causes convection to occur, resulting in storms that often blanket the planet with dust. The dust absorbs sunlight, further warming the atmosphere. When Mars is farthest from the Sun, there are fewer temperature differences and the weather is calmer. This results in two distinct summer seasons: a warm, dusty southern summer and a cold, dust-free northern summer.

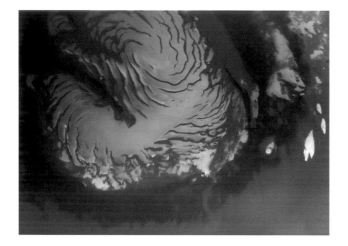

This is the north polar cap in early northern summer. The light-toned surfaces are residual water ice that remains through the summer season. The circular band of dark material surrounding the cap consists mainly of sand dunes formed by wind. (NASA/JPL/Malin Space Science Systems)

Facing page: As the Sun sets over the Martian south polar region, its light passes through layers of carbon dioxide and water ice crystals, creating beautiful glowing halos.

The northern seasonal cap, which is made mostly of carbon dioxide, forms when the atmosphere is filled with dust from summer storms. The dust gets mixed with the carbon dioxide as it freezes onto the surface, so the northern seasonal cap is darker. The southern seasonal cap forms when the atmosphere has much less dust in it, so it is brighter. The northern cap is the larger of the two—its diameter of 600 miles (965 km) is almost three times larger than the 220-mile (350-km)-wide southern cap.

The temperatures differ, too, with the southern cap being the coldest. While summer in the southern hemisphere is warmer than summer in the northern hemisphere, winters in the south are much, much colder, resulting in a southern cap that does not melt as much as the northern cap does in the summer. The southern cap also contains more water ice than the northern cap because the extremely cold temperatures have prevented the water ice there—which has a higher melting point than carbon dioxide—from evaporating.

One question that puzzled astronomers ever since the polar caps were discovered is: How thick are they? Originally, most astronomers thought they had to be very thin, perhaps no more than a heavy coating of frost on the ground. Now we know, from measurements made by spacecraft, that the caps are fairly substantial. The permanent water ice cap that lies beneath the seasonal carbon dioxide cap is heavy enough that it never melts.

The landscapes of the polar regions are among the most interesting on the planet. The poles are buried under thick layers of sediments, laid down by millions of years of wind-carried dust.

Dust and volcanic ash deposited over millions of years lies in layers surrounding the polar caps. Erosion has exposed these layers as meandering terraces, like enormous stairs.

Cutting through these deposits are winding valleys that curl out from around the poles.

Surrounding the north polar cap is a band, or collar, of very dark terrain. This band becomes more visible in the summer as the ice retreats and the cap gets smaller. In the nineteenth and early twentieth centuries, this was thought to be one of the main pieces of evidence for large amounts of water on Mars. Astronomers thought that the dark color was caused by water flowing from the melting poles, or perhaps even vegetation enjoying the moist soil. Today we know that the dark region is actually a vast sea of sand dunes.

The broad valleys that spiral away from the poles reveal step-like terraces on their slopes. Over millions of years, fine dust deposited by storms and ash from volcanic eruptions have built up layers hundreds of feet deep. Within these layers are buried layers of water and carbon dioxide ice. Wind erosion of the soil and evaporation of the ice has created hundreds of miles of meandering terraces rising in gracefully curving 90-foot (30-m) steps. They are constantly changing shape and direction as wind erosion and evaporation continue.

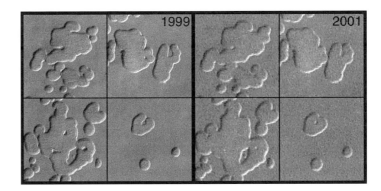

Over a period of less than two years, the *Mars Global Surveyor* observed these changes in the landscape around the south pole. As subsurface ice and frozen carbon dioxide evaporate in the summer, the landscape above collapses and erodes. (NASA/JPL/Malin Space Science Systems)

When the *Viking 1* orbiter began mapping Mars in 1976, an interesting image was received at the Jet Propulsion Laboratory in Pasadena, California. It showed a surface feature resembling a human or apelike face. The photo was immediately released to the public as an interesting geological feature and dubbed the "Face on Mars," which NASA soon realized was probably a mistake.

Although scientists knew that it was nothing but a trick of shadows on a complex rock formation, many people thought that it was an artificial structure, much like the Sphinx in Egypt, and was proof of life on Mars. Some speculated that it had been built in the distant past and others thought that it was evidence that Martians were still living on the planet. Whole books were written about the mysterious Face on Mars, and there were Web sites and movies (such as *Mission to Mars*, 2000). But the people who jumped to such wild conclusions didn't account for the fact that the photo wasn't a very good one at all. The "face" was only a very, very small part of a much larger photo, which in turn was of only moderate resolution, so that when the "face" is enlarged enough to see, the image is of very low quality. Saying that there is actually a "face" there is as valid as saying that the animals and figures you might see in the shapes of clouds are *really* there.

Scientists were sure that as soon as higher-quality images could be obtained, the "face" would disappear. And they were right. When the *Mars Global Surveyor* obtained very high-resolution images of the area, the "face" was revealed to be what astronomers were sure of all along: a mesa with a wild jumble of broken rocks on top.

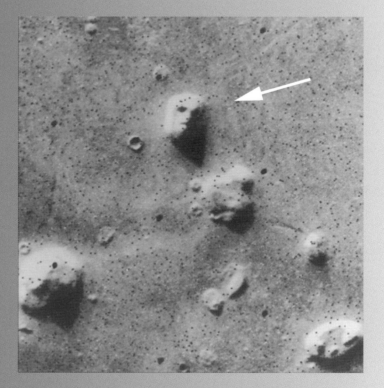

The original photo of the "Face on Mars" (NASA/JPL)

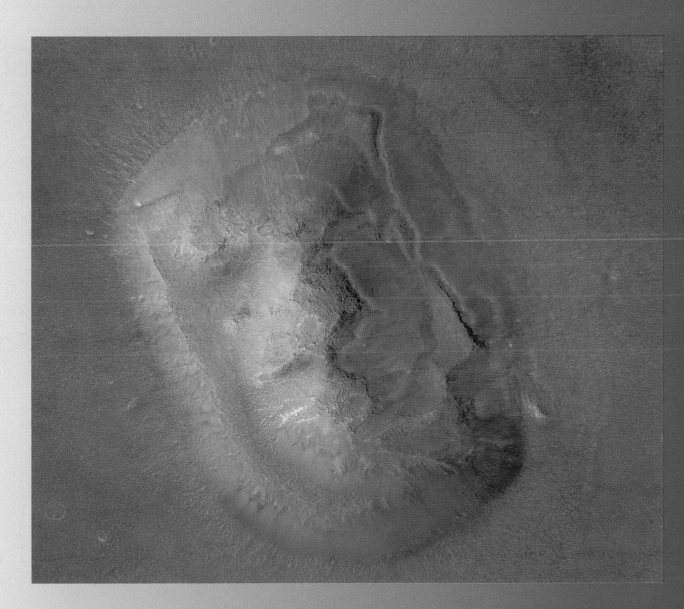

The "face" disappeared in higher-quality photos. (NASA/JPL/Malin Space Science Systems)

CHAPTER EIGHT

THE MOONS

Astronomers knew since 1877 that the two moons of Mars, Phobos and Deimos, were tiny bodies, but no one knew what they looked like until the first spacecraft photos of them were beamed back to Earth. The photos revealed a pair of dark, cratered, potato-shaped rocks.

Phobos is distinguished by a very large crater—named Stickney, the maiden name of Mrs. Asaph Hall, to honor her encouragement of her husband's search for the moons. Stickney is 5 miles (8 km) wide, which is a huge hole in a tiny moon that measures only 17 by 12 miles (27 by 19 km). If the impact that created Stickney had been any larger, it might have broken the moon into pieces.

A peculiar feature of Phobos is the many grooves that stretch around the little moon. Some of them are as wide as 300 feet (100 m) and as long as 6 miles (10 km). Since they seem to radiate away from Stickney, they may be fractures caused by the impact that created the crater.

This is a view of Mars seen from its inner moon, Phobos, which orbits only 3,720 miles (6,000 km) above the surface of Mars. From this distance, the giant volcano Olympus Mons, as well as several other volcanoes, can be seen clearly.

Phobos as photographed by the *Viking* orbiter: The large crater is Stickney and the parallel grooves below the crater may be cracks caused by the impact that created it. (NASA/JPL)

THE MOONS OF MARS

NAME	DATE OF DISCOVERY	DISTANCE FROM MARS*	SIZE †
Phobos	1877	5,827 miles (9,377 km)	17 x 12 miles (28 x 19 km)
Deimos	1877	14,579 miles (23,462 km)	10 x 6 miles (16 x 10 km)

* As measured from the center of Mars.

† Mars's moons are not spherical. In this case, the longest and narrowest dimensions are given.

Many scientists believe that Phobos is doomed. It is so close to Mars that the thin outer atmosphere of Mars is causing Phobos's orbit to slowly decay. In a few million years Phobos will crash into the planet.

Deimos, the smaller moon, looks very different from Phobos, except for the similarity in color. Deimos is much smoother, with far fewer craters, though it has many boulders scattered around its surface. Its gravity is so weak that if you were to drop a rock from eye level it would take nearly thirty seconds to hit the ground—fifty times longer than a rock dropped on Earth. An astronaut could throw a baseball into orbit around it!

Seen from the surface of Mars, neither moon would look very interesting. Because they are so small, even the nearer one,

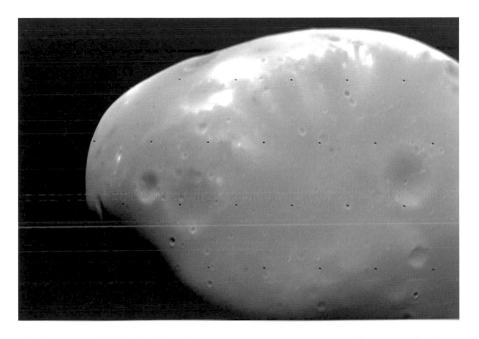

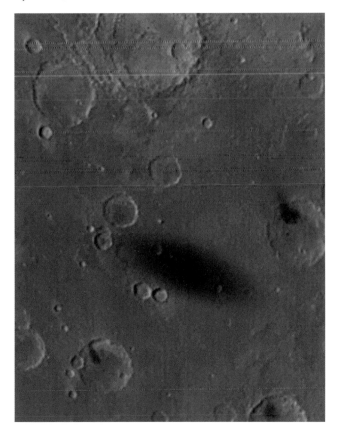

Left: Deimos as seen by the *Viking* orbiter: It is not only smaller than Phobos, but much smoother with fewer craters. (NASA/JPL) Below: The shadow of Phobos was caught racing across the Martian landscape in this *Mars Global Surveyor* photograph. (NASA/JPL/Malin Space Science Systems)

Phobos, would look like little more than an especially large, bright star, and Deimos would be only a bright point of light. But their *speed* would set them apart from the stars in the night sky.

Phobos orbits Mars in less than a Martian day. It takes only 7.7 hours to circle Mars once. Since a day on Mars is about 24 hours, this means that Phobos orbits Mars faster than the planet rotates. The result is that, unlike Earth's Moon, Phobos rises in the west and sets in the east. As the planet rotates, the surface of Mars moves in the same direction as Phobos, so the moon actually completes a little more than two revolutions every day, with just 11.1 hours between one moonrise and the next one. But once Phobos has risen, it takes only 4.38 hours to rush through the sky and set again.

The Sun is disappearing behind the vast bulk of Mars in this scene set on the tiny inner moon, Phobos. Sunlight, which has been reddened by passing though the dust-laden atmosphere of Mars, illuminates the surface of Phobos with a coppery glow.

ANOTHER MYSTERY OF MARS'S MOONS

In *Gulliver's Travels* (1762), Jonathan Swift wrote about the moons of Mars:

> They [the Laputians] have likewise discovered two lesser Stars, or Satellites, which revolve about Mars, whereof the innermost is distant from the Center of the primary Planet exactly three of his Diameters, and the outermost five; the former revolves in the space of ten Hours, and the latter in Twenty-one and a Half; so that the Squares of their periodical Times, are very near in the same proportion with the Cubes of their Distance from the Center of Mars; which evidently shows them to be governed by the same Law of Gravitation, that influences the other heavenly Bodies.

This is an almost perfect description of the orbits of Phobos and Deimos. What makes it remarkable is that it was written in 1726, a century and a half before Asaph Hall discovered them! How did Swift know there were two moons? How did he know that the innermost moon circled Mars in less than one Martian day? Especially since this latter fact is unique in the solar system—no other moon circles its planet faster than its planet rotates. Was his description just a coincidence or did Swift have some inside knowledge? Nobody really knows.

Deimos, on the other hand, orbits Mars in 30.3 hours, only about 6 hours longer than a Martian day. It would appear to an observer on the surface to hang almost motionless in the sky, imperceptibly creeping across. More than 60 hours must pass between Deimos-rise and Deimos-set.

The view of Mars from its moons would be far more impressive than the view of the moons seen from their planet. From Deimos, Mars would resemble a huge reddish-orange beach ball more than thirty times larger than a full Moon seen from Earth. But the view from Phobos would be even more spectacular. Mars would *be* Phobos's sky, looming more than eighty times larger than a full Moon back on Earth.

One of the many mysteries about the two little moons is their origin. Were they formed in orbit around Mars? Are they the remnants of a larger moon that was broken up by a massive impact? A Russian astronomer once made the astonishing claim that the moons were really space stations launched into orbit by Martians! One possible clue to their origin is that they are both very dark, darker than an asphalt parking lot, resembling the carbon-rich meteorites known as **carbonaceous chondrites**. These are common in the asteroid belt, so it may be that Phobos and Deimos are captured asteroids. Both moons do look very much like the close-up photos of asteroids that have been visited by spacecraft in recent years.

CHAPTER NINE

LIFE ON MARS?

Back in the 1950s, when the U.S. space program was just beginning, Lee DuBridge, the science adviser to President Eisenhower, recognized the importance of looking for life elsewhere in the universe. "Either we are alone or we are not," he said. "Either way boggles the mind."

People have been wondering about the possibilities of life on other worlds ever since the discovery that there *were* other worlds. Soon after Galileo's announcement that Venus, Jupiter, and Mars were worlds like Earth, many books speculated on just what the inhabitants of these worlds might be like. Early science fiction novels took their readers on adventurous journeys to these strange new lands. As far back as 1686, the French mathematician Bernard de Fontenelle published *Discourses on the Plurality of Worlds*. In this book, a strange mixture of very little science and much speculation, he wondered how Earth was created and whether there might be other inhabited planets out there. To make up for what he thought would be dark, moonless nights on Mars, de Fontenelle said there must be glowing mountains and luminescent birds.

(75)

This illustration accompanied a 1907 magazine article by H.G. Wells. It shows what Wells thought Martians might look like, according to the conditions on the planet as they were known at the time. They had large chests because of the thin air, feathers to help keep them warm, and slender limbs because of the weak gravity.

Most early writers were aware that the conditions on other worlds would produce creatures very different from those on Earth. In 1698, Christian Huygens suggested that Martians would be covered by fur and feathers. In 1758, the Swedish mystic and philosopher Emanuel Swedenborg said that Martians must be gentle beings who dressed in tree bark. The anonymous author of *Fantastical Excursions into the Planets* (1839) believed that the size, mass, gravity, and climate of other worlds suggested a wide variety of possible life forms. In spite of these writers and others like them, most people before the twentieth century believed that Martians would be more or less human in appearance. It took H.G. Wells's horrifying novel *The War of the Worlds* (1898) to introduce the idea of monstrous, inhuman, hostile aliens.

But why pick on Mars? Of all the planets in the solar system, why has Mars always been the first suspect when people talk about life on other worlds? Even the phrase "little green man from Mars" has become a cliché signifying any alien creature. This is because among all the planets, Mars appears to be the most Earthlike. It has an atmosphere, polar caps, clouds, and—at least to early viewers—signs of "vegetation" in the seasonal changing of color. Percival Lowell's theories convinced the average reader that Mars had not only supported life in the past but was still home to an active, if dying, civilization.

Even if astronomers were not quite so convinced about the possibility of canal-building Martians, the idea of life of some kind existing on Mars certainly seemed possible. Rightly or wrongly, the search for life elsewhere in the solar system has always concentrated on the red planet. (Today Mars is rivaled by Jupiter's moon, Europa, as the object of the search for life. Many astronomers believe that life may have evolved in the deep, warm ocean they think exists beneath the Europan ice crust.)

Until the *Viking* landers set down on the Martian deserts in 1976, the debate was not whether there was life on Mars, but what kind of life it might be. Many scientists were so certain that the landers would detect signs of life that what actually happened was a complete surprise.

Experiments on Mars

The two *Viking* landers were specifically intended to search for life, with five experiments specially designed to look for signs of biological activity. The results raised more questions—and started more debates—than they answered. Two of the experiments were negative, but the remaining three were ambiguous. The first and second experiments, the *Viking* cameras and the soil analyzer, were designed to look for the remnants of life. The cameras showed nothing that suggested that life had ever existed on Mars, let alone in the present day. The experiment designed to analyze soil samples found no organic molecules.

The other three experiments, however, were designed to look for ongoing biological activity, such as photosynthesis—the process by which plants use sunlight to convert food into energy. To do this, the probe placed soil samples into special chambers. Nutrients were added and the instruments watched to see what happened. Certain changes would indicate the presence of living organisms. All three tests were positive!

For more than two hundred years, astronomers had observed color changes on the surface of Mars. It seemed to them that the dusky areas looked distinctly greenish, and many astronomers believed that the color became greener during the spring and summer and browner in the fall and winter—just as might be expected if the dark areas were in fact vegetation. It turned out, however, that the apparent color was just an optical illusion—much in the same way that the canals turned out to be an illusion. The color of the dark areas is actually a neutral brownish-gray. Seen next to the bright orangish deserts, contrast made the dark areas seem greenish, since green is the complementary color of orange. You can get an idea of how this happens by staring at the orange square below for thirty seconds and then moving your gaze to the blank area next to it. You will see a green square—the after-image of the orange one.

But once their initial excitement passed, scientists began to question the results of the experiments. They suspected that the findings might be the result of unexpected chemical processes instead of life. It was possible, they suggested, that the **ultraviolet radiation** that bathes the Martian surface, which has no ozone layer to protect it from this dangerous form of light, created different properties in the minerals that made up the soil. These altered minerals might have caused the reactions that were observed in the experiments.

So, while *Viking* didn't find any definite signs of life, neither did it prove there *is* no life on Mars. It may be, many scientists suggested, that there is life on Mars and the *Viking* landers just couldn't find it. After all, they explored only a very tiny part of the planet—and Mars has more dry land than Earth. What if, for instance, in order to escape the deadly ultraviolet radiation, life had retreated deeper beneath the surface than the few inches the *Vikings* were able to dig? Other scientists pointed out that *Viking*-type experiments failed to find signs of life in Antarctic soil samples, where microorganisms were known to exist.

The whole question of life on Mars—whether it ever existed in the past and if it might still exist—really hinges on water. For life to exist—at least life as we know it—liquid water is necessary, since it is a vital component of the biochemistry of all known living organisms. Did Mars ever have large amounts of water in the past? Does any water still exist on the planet? The riverlike channels discovered by *Mariner 9* suggest that Mars may have had vast quantities of water millions of years ago. But if this was true, what happened to it? This question may have been recently answered.

In 2002, NASA's *Mars Global Surveyor* spacecraft photographed features that suggest there may be sources of liquid water existing today at or near the surface. The new images show features similar to those left by flash floods on Earth, gullies formed by flowing water, and deposits of soil and rocks transported by these flows. The features appear to be so young that they might have been formed very recently. Scientists studying these images think they may be evidence of a supply of groundwater. This is believed to be about 300 to 1,300 feet (100 to 400 m) below the surface. The water that flowed down each of the many gullies may have had a volume of about 90,000 cubic feet (about 2,500 m³)—

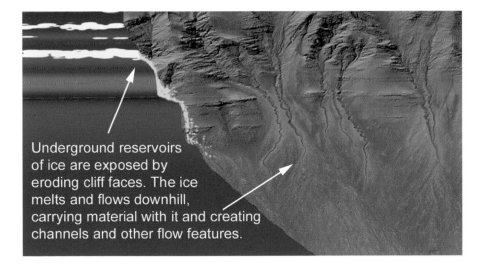

Underground reservoirs of ice are exposed by eroding cliff faces. The ice melts and flows downhill, carrying material with it and creating channels and other flow features.

When an underground layer of ice is exposed in the face of a cliff or crater rim, it melts and causes many different types of runoff features, such as the channels and deltas seen on the right.

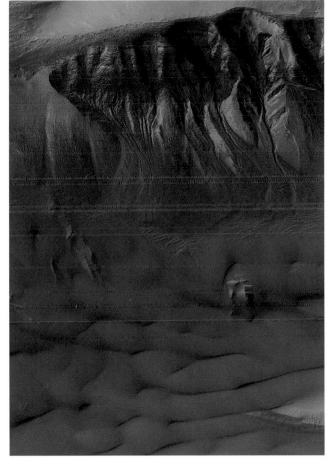

The effects possibly caused by flowing water can be seen clearly in this spectacular view of a cliff where water from melting ice might have streamed downhill, cutting hundreds of winding channels. (NASA/JPL/Malin Space Science Systems)

enough water to sustain one hundred average homes for a month or fill seven community-sized swimming pools.

In 2004 scientists were excited about the discovery of methane gas on Mars. Since atmospheric methane rapidly decomposes, it must be constantly replaced. If there is methane in the atmosphere on Mars, there must be some source providing a steady supply of the gas. Much of the methane in Earth's atmosphere is produced as a biological waste product. Some of Earth's methane also comes from nonbiological sources, such as volcanoes. So the question remains: Is the methane on Mars produced by living organisms, or does it come from volcanic sources? The discovery of methane has only added fuel to the debate about life on the red planet.

Two more discoveries that suggest the possibility of life on Mars were actually found on Earth. One was the discovery of life forms existing in extremely hostile environments—environments even more hostile than any of those that might be expected on Mars. These organisms, called **extremophiles**, live in areas on Earth that are so acid, salty, poisonous, hot, or cold that any ordinary plant or animal would die. Many scientists believe that if life could evolve and flourish in such hostile conditions on Earth, it might be possible for life to have also evolved on Mars, especially if conditions on Mars in the distant past were more temperate.

The other discovery came from the study of certain meteorites found on Earth that are believed to have been blasted off the surface of Mars by asteroid impacts. Many of the meteorites show the effects of water on the minerals that compose them, suggesting that they were exposed to liquid water at some time

ALH84001,0

0.4"
(1 cm)

Scientists believe that this meteorite, which fell on Earth, originally came from Mars. (NASA)

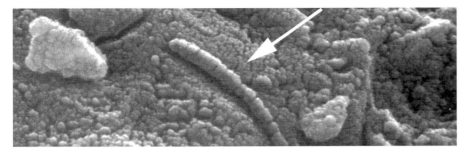

Some scientists believe that this microscopic feature, found inside a meteorite, may be a fossilized Martian life form (NASA)

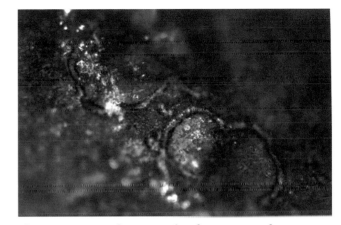

This is a microphotograph of a strange feature found in a Martian meteorite. Some scientists believe that it may be the fossil remains of an organism that might once have lived on Mars. Other scientists argue that it is only a mineral deposit. (NASA/JPL)

during their existence on Mars. In 1996 a team of scientists startled the world by announcing that they'd found signs of fossilized bacteria in one of the meteorites. Many other scientists, however, argued against this discovery, saying that the "fossils" were nothing more than mineral formations. There were, however, traces of a substance called magnetite, which is formed only by biological organisms. This added fuel to the argument that the meteor contained the fossilized remains of living creatures, though many scientists debate the importance of the magnetite.

The evidence for not just trace amounts of water but vast quantities of it—as well as the discovery of organisms on Earth capable of existing in the hostile Martian environment—has added new fuel to the ancient desire to explore Mars. Inspired by the possibility of finding life on the red planet, scores of missions are now planned, with intentions of landing humans on the planet before 2020.

Either we are alone in the universe or we are not. Those are the only two possibilities. Which would you prefer it to be?

CHAPTER TEN

FUTURE MARS

Mars is already one of the most explored planets in the solar system. More than thirty space probes have been sent there, though only about a dozen have been successful. The fact that so much effort has been expended in spite of such difficulties is some indication of how important we consider the planet to be.

A great many more probes are planned for the near future. The recent discoveries made by the *Mars Global Surveyor*—especially the discovery of possible large amounts of water on Mars—have spurred even more interest than ever. The European Space Agency (ESA) sent a lander, the *Beagle 2*, to Mars in 2003 as part of its Mars Express program. One of its main objectives is the search for signs of life. France plans to send its *Mars Reconnaissance Orbiter* to the red planet in 2005, and this will return extremely high-resolution images of the surface.

Five different missions are proposed for 2007, including NASA's "small scout missions," which will deploy a number of small, automatic landers, aircraft, and balloons that will range all over the planet. An international mission headed by NASA and

(82)

France plans to launch the first Mars sample return probe in 2011. This will bring the first samples of rocks and soil from the Martian surface back to Earth in 2014.

In spite of these and the many other exciting missions being planned for the next two decades, one question remains: When will human beings land on Mars?

Sending a mission to Mars would be a complex project to say the least—many times more difficult than sending astronauts to the Moon. Over the years there have been many different plans for sending humans to the red planet, all of which have their special merits and drawbacks. Some of these have been proposed by NASA while others have been suggested by aerospace companies and individual scientists and engineers.

The questions about sending humans to Mars range from the type of spacecraft that needs to be used, to the assurance of crew safety and the resources and equipment required, to the time that should be spent on Mars, and much, much more. Every aspect of the mission must be studied in detail before a mission to Mars is launched because there would be no way to help the astronauts if something were to go wrong. Once they leave Earth, the crew must be completely self-sufficient. They need to be flexible enough to adapt to new situations and unexpected emergencies. The crew must also make the final decision on what landing site to choose, because they will have the most up-to-date information on Mars's weather conditions.

There would be a lot for human explorers to do on Mars. Even though the planet is only half the diameter of Earth, it has more land area, because three quarters of Earth's surface is covered with water.

The remaining land area on Earth is in fact less than the total surface area of Mars—none of which is covered by water. That is a lot of territory to explore!

A human mission to Mars lies on the very edge of present technology and engineering. Committing to it would be the most ambitious project any country could undertake. It might be such a large, expensive project that no individual country could handle it. A successful mission to Mars might have to be an international undertaking, combining the resources and capabilities of many different countries. Would it be worthwhile? Only going to Mars can really answer that question. It is certain, though, that in giving us a better understanding of Mars, such a mission would help us better understand the Earth we live on, and perhaps even how life began.

Facing page: The Twin Peaks in the background are low hills to the southwest of the *Mars Pathfinder* landing site. They are approximately 98 to 115 feet high (30 to 35 m). North Twin (right) is approximately 2,800 feet (860 m) from the lander, and South Twin (left) is about 3,300 feet (1,006 m) away. The scene includes bouldery piles of debris from ancient flooding. (NASA/JPL)

TERRAFORMING MARS

Instead of humans adapting themselves to live on Mars—by constructing special habitats and wearing spacesuits—an even more ambitious idea is to adapt Mars to suit human beings. It might be possible, suggest many scientists, to change the present conditions on Mars. Instead of being a frigid planet with no breathable atmosphere and all of its water locked up in underground ice, it might be transformed into a planet more resembling Earth. Changing a planet in this way is called **terraforming**. The discovery that there are vast underground reservoirs of ice on Mars makes this idea possible, for the ice is not only a source of water but of oxygen, which is necessary for a breathable atmosphere, and hydrogen, which can be used as fuel.

One way in which Mars might be terraformed would require the melting of the southern polar ice cap. This would release huge quantities of carbon dioxide (CO_2) into the atmosphere. Since CO_2 is a greenhouse gas, it would trap heat from the Sun, and the planet would begin to grow warmer. This would release more CO_2 from the surface and maybe even melt the northern polar ice cap. The release of CO_2 and water vapor into the atmosphere would also raise the air pressure. This would allow liquid water to form on the surface. Once this was done, widespread plant life could start enriching the atmosphere with oxygen via photosynthesis.

If humans ever undertake such a vast project they would have to be patient: It might take as long as 10,000 years to transform Mars into an Earthlike world. But there may be more than technological difficulties facing the terraforming of Mars. Many people have questioned the wisdom of doing something that would change the face of an entire planet forever. After all, they ask, if there can be environmental, scientific, and moral objections to flooding a valley by building a dam across a river, what about changing an entire world? The word *terraforming* literally means forming another world into a duplicate of Earth—Mars as we know it would no longer exist.

Someday, if Mars is ever terraformed, it may have lakes, oceans, and an atmosphere dense enough to support human life. In this view from Deimos of the future Mars, much of the northern hemisphere is covered by a shallow ocean, craters have become lakes, and the great Mariner Valley (left, going into the shadow) is a river. (Miller/Space-Graphics)

GLOSSARY

accretion: the process by which planetesimals accumulate into larger bodies.

aphelion: the point in a planet's orbit when it is farthest from the Sun.

AU (astronomical unit): the average distance of Earth from the Sun—92,957,130 miles (149,600,000 km).

axis (*plural* axes): the imaginary line around which a planet or other body rotates.

caldera: a large crater formed by the explosion or collapse of a volcanic vent.

carbonaceous chondrite: a meteor containing a large amount of carbon.

chaotic terrain: jumbled, rugged landscapes often caused by the melting of underground ice.

differentiation: a process during the early formation of a planet when heavy metals sink toward the center and lighter materials float toward the surface.

elliptical: oval-shaped.

extremophile: an organism living in an unusually hostile environment.

magma: lava while still underground.

mantle: the region between the core and the outer crust of a planet.

mons (*plural* montes): mountain.

patera: a shallow crater with a complex, scalloped rim.

perihelion: the point in a planet's orbit when it is nearest the Sun.

planetesimal: small rocky and metallic bodies that accrete into larger bodies, such as planets.

plate tectonics: geologic forces that cause the crust of a planet to shift.

protoplanetary disk: a disk of dust and gas surrounding a star that may eventually form a planetary system.

protostar: a sphere of gas that has collapsed far enough to become hot but not yet hot enough to start the process of nuclear fusion.

rover: a small, robotic probe capable of moving around on the surface of a planet or moon.

shield volcano: a volcano built up by steady, slow outflow of lava and ash; usually cone-shaped with low, sloping sides.

star: a mass of gaseous material that's massive enough to initiate nuclear reactions in its core.

sublimate: ice or other solids turning directly into a gas without first going through a liquid stage.

terra: an extensive land mass.

terraforming: transforming a planet into one more resembling Earth.

tholus: a small dome-shaped mountain or hill.

ultraviolet radiation: an energetic form of light invisible to the human eye.

valles (*singular* **vallis**): sinuous valleys.

Books

Beatty, J. Kelly, Carolyn Collins Petersen, and Andrew Chaikin, eds. *The New Solar System*. Cambridge, MA: Sky Publishing, 1999.

Bone, Neil. *Mars Observer's Guide*. Toronto: Firefly Books, 2003.

Boyce, Joseph. *The Smithsonian Book of Mars*. Washington, D.C.: Smithsonian Institution Press, 2002.

Crossman, Frank. *On to Mars*. Burlington, Ontario: Apogee Books, 2002.

Godwin, Robert. *Mars—The NASA Mission Reports*. Burlington, Ontario: Apogee Books, 2000.

Hartmann, William K. *Moons and Planets*. Belmont, CA: Wadsworth Publishing, 1999.

———. *Traveler's Guide to Mars*. New York: Workman Publishing, 2003.

Miller, Ron, and William K. Hartmann. *The Grand Tour*. New York: Workman Publishing, 1993.

Morton, Oliver. *Mapping Mars*. New York: Picador USA, 2002.

Scagell, Robine. *The New Book of Space*. Brookfield, CT: Copper Beech, 1997.

Schaaf, Fred. *Planetology*. Danbury, CT: Franklin Watts, 1996.

Sheehan, William. *The Planet Mars: A History of Observation and Discovery*. Tucson: University of Arizona Press, 1996.

Sheehan, William, and Stephen James O'Meara. *Mars: The Lure of the Red Planet*. Amherst, NY: Prometheus Books, 2001.

Great Fiction about Mars

Mars has inspired more writers than any other planet. Here is a selection of some of the best stories written between 1900 and today:

Bear, Greg. *Moving Mars*. New York: Tor Books, 1994.

Benford, Gregory. *The Martian Race*. New York: Aspect, 2001.

Bova, Ben. *Mars*. New York: Bantam, 1993.

Bradbury, Ray. *The Martian Chronicles*. New York: Avon, 1997 (Originally published in 1950).

Burroughs, Edgar Rice. *A Princess of Mars*. New York: Ballantine, 1990 (Originally published in 1917, this is the first book in a series of adventure novels that take place on a Mars inspired by Percival Lowell's books).

Disch, Thomas M. *The Brave Little Toaster Goes to Mars*. New York: Doubleday, 1983.

Hartmann, William K. *Mars Underground*. New York: Tor Books, 1999.

Heinlein, Robert A. *Red Planet*. New York: Ballantine, 1991 (Originally published in 1949).

Robinson, Kim Stanley. *Red Mars*. New York: Bantam, 1993.

———. *Green Mars*. New York: Bantam, 1995.

———. *Blue Mars*. New York: Bantam, 1997.

Wells, H.G. *The War of the Worlds*. New York: Bantam, 1988 (Originally published in 1898).

Magazines

Astronomy
www.astronomy.com

Sky & Telescope
www.skypub.com

Organizations

American Astronomical Society
2000 Florida Avenue NW, Suite 400
Washington, D.C. 20009-1231
www.AAS.org

Association of Lunar and Planetary Observers
P.O. Box 13456
Springfield, IL 62791-3456
www.lpl.arizona.edu/alpo/

Astronomical Society of the Pacific
390 Ashton Avenue
San Francisco, CA 94112
www.astrosociety.org

The Planetary Society
65 N. Catalina Avenue
Pasadena, CA 91106-2301
planetary.org

Web sites

Daily Martian Weather Report
www-star.stanford.edu/projects/mgs/dmwr.html
A report on the weather on Mars that is updated daily, with maps and photos.

Exploring Mars
www.exploringmars.com
An excellent introduction to the planet.

Malin Space Science Systems
barsoom.msss.com/
The source for the latest pictures and information from the *Mars Global Surveyor* mission.

Mars Exploration Rover Mission
marsrovers.jpl.nasa.gov/home/
The official site for news and photos from the Mars Rover mission.

Mars Express
sci.esa.int/marsexpress/
The official site for the Mars Express mission.

The Mars Society
www.marssociety.org/
A Web site that advocates human exploration of Mars.

Mars Today
www.fourmilab.ch/cgi-bin/
uncgi/Yourtel?aim=4&z=1
A Web site showing where to find Mars in the night sky.

NASA Spacelink
spacelink.msfc.nasa.gov/index.html
A gateway to many NASA Web sites about the Sun and planets.

Nine Planets
www.nineplanets.org
Detailed information about the Sun, the planets, and all the moons, including many photos and useful links to other Web sites.

Solar System Simulator
space.jpl.nasa.gov/
An amazing Web site that allows visitors to travel to all the planets and moons and create their own views of these distant worlds.

Hugo Award–winner Ron Miller is an illustrator and author who specializes in astronomy. He has created or contributed to many books on the subject, including *Cycles of Fire*, *The History of Earth*, and *The Grand Tour*. Among his nonfiction books for young people are *The History of Rockets* and *The History of Science Fiction*, as well as the Worlds Beyond series, which was awarded the 2003 American Institute of Physics Science Writing Award in Physics and Astronomy (Children's) for the first four books—*Extrasolar Planets*, *The Sun*, *Jupiter*, and *Venus*. Miller's work has won many awards and distinctions, including the 2002 Hugo Award for Best Non-Fiction for *The Art of Chesley Bonestell*. He has designed a set of ten commemorative stamps on the planets in our solar system for the U.S. Postal Service. He has written several novels and has worked on a number of science fiction films, such as *Dune* and *Total Recall*. His original paintings can be found in collections all over the world, including that of the National Air and Space Museum in Washington, D.C., and magazines such as *National Geographic*, *Scientific American*, *Sky and Telescope*, and *Natural History*. Miller lives in King George, Virginia, with his wife and cats.